A CATHOLIC BOOK OF THE MASS

Holy Transfiguration Monastery

The Monks of Mt. Tabor
(Byzantine-Ukrainian Catholic)

17001 Tomki Rd., Redwood Valley, CA 95470
(707) 485-8959

A CATHOLIC BOOK OF THE MASS

Rev. William Ogrodowski

Our Sunday Visitor, Inc.
Huntington, Indiana 46750

Nihil Obstat:
Rev. Frank C. Sokol, Ph.D.
Censor Librorum

Imprimatur:
✠Anthony J. Bevilacqua, D.D., M.A., J.C.D., J.D.
Bishop of Pittsburgh
March 15, 1985

The Nihil Obstat and Imprimatur are official declarations that a book or pamphlet is free of doctrinal or moral error. No implication is contained therein that those who have granted the Nihil Obstat or Imprimatur agree with the contents, opinions or statements expressed.

Excerpts from conciliar documents are reprinted by permission from *The Documents of Vatican II* (Walter M. Abbott, S.J., general editor), copyright © 1966 by The America Press. All rights reserved. Brief excerpts from Holy Scripture are mostly from *The Jerusalem Bible*, copyright © 1966, 1967 and 1968 by Darton, Longman & Todd Ltd and Doubleday & Company, Inc., and *The New American Bible*, copyright © 1969, 1970 by the Confraternity of Christian Doctrine, Washington, D.C. All rights reserved. The author also wishes to acknowledge the contributions of all authors and publishers listed in the notes and bibliographies at the end of this book.

Library of Congress Catalogue No: 84-60752
ISBN 0-87973-600-3

Cover design by Rebecca J. O'Brien

Printed in the United States of America

Dedication

*To the faculty and students of Saint Paul Seminary,
Pittsburgh, Pennsylvania, in grateful appreciation
for the constant support and encouragement shown me
during the completion of this book.*

Abbreviations Used in This Book
(Documents of and since Vatican Council II)

DV: *Dei Verbum* (Dogmatic Constitution on Divine Revelation)

GI: General Instruction on the *Roman Missal* (Sacramentary)

GS: *Gaudium et Spes* (Pastoral Constitution on the Church in the Modern World)

LG: *Lumen Gentium* (Dogmatic Constitution on the Church)

MF: *Mysterium Fidei* (Encyclical Letter of Pope Paul VI on the Holy Eucharist)

PO: *Presbyterorum Ordinis* (Decree on the Ministry and Life of Priests)

SC: *Sacrosanctum Concilium* (Constitution on the Sacred Liturgy)

UR: *Unitatis Redintegratio* (Decree on Ecumenism)

Contents

Foreword

The 1985 extraordinary assembly of the Synod of Bishops was convoked by Pope John Paul II to examine the progress that the Church is making in the renewal called for by the Second Vatican Council. Is the Church, in her members, growing and thriving spiritually today?

The first major effort of the Council in apportioning her energy in this renewal was the reform of the liturgy. The Constitution on the Sacred Liturgy was the most immediate fruit of the Second Vatican Council. It was also the logical starting point for general renewal in the Mystical Body because the principal liturgical celebration is the Eucharist.

By its very nature, the Eucharist is a renewal. In it we celebrate the sacred mysteries of our death and resurrection to new life in Christ. Every time Jesus is made present again in the breaking of the bread, the world is somehow changed. It is made fresh and alive again. But the Eucharist is not to be considerd solely a sanctuary event. If its real force is to be felt, the Eucharist must be understood and experienced as the very apex of Christ's redeeming action throughout the whole worshiping community. All present at the celebration should fully share — participate — in the wondrous event that is Christ really and truly, body and blood, soul and divinity, present with His people.

Every liturgical commemoration of Christ is as new as was Jesus in Nazareth 2,000 years ago. Each celebration of the Lord starts all over again the wonders of the Teacher of Galilee. Every

Mass represents anew the love of Calvary. This remarkable representation of the Savior is the work of the Church and, therefore, of all her members. Every believer is a living witness to the presence and love of God's only Son.

The Council repeats what has always been the living Christian tradition. We must first ourselves know Christ if we would have others see Him in us. "It is the function of the Church, led by the Holy Spirit who renews and purifies her ceaselessly, to make God the Father and His incarnate Son present and as it were visible. This result is achieved chiefly by the witness of a living and mature faith" (Church in the Modern World, 21).

The Eucharist, naturally, forms the core of any such witness. Every time the Lord made present is received in Communion, He comes again to initiate His witness. He tells us, the world, and His Father of His great love. And He passes on to us a share in His love. In doing so, He consecrates each disciple with the mission to make known to all the world a love so great that it "emptied itself" to become one with us and die for us.

Initiation and conviction are the cornerstones of true witness. The Mass enlivens both. It renews the initiation of the believer into the mystery of Christ's death and resurrection. It is the primary daily source of incorporation into Jesus Christ. But a proper liturgy also strengthens the conviction of the believer. Full participation in the revealing word of God leads each worshiper to a heightened awareness of God's plan for each of us.

The "good tree" of the New Testament thrives on the Eucharist. Only in it and through it can any fruitful witness take place. It is, then, no wonder that the Church has seen and continues to see in the celebration of the Eucharistic Liturgy — the Mass — the source of all good fruit and new life.

Father William Ogrodowski has provided us a thoughtful guide to full participation in the joy and renewal of the Mass. With insight and scholarship, he treats the various aspects of our rich sharing in the mystery that is the Eucharist.

So complex and deep is the celebration we call the Mass that it can be viewed from many angles. Thanks to Father Ogrodowski's efforts, we are all given various starting points from which to arrive at a more complete understanding of the center of the life of the Church. This work is a useful tool for students, an excellent textbook, fine source material and, perhaps most importantly, a beautiful meditation on the mystery of the death and resurrection of Jesus Christ as we share in it through our full participation in the Mass.

> Reverend Donald W. Wuerl
> Rector
> Saint Paul Seminary
> Pittsburgh Pennsylvania

Feast of St. John Bosco
January 31, 1985

CHAPTER ONE

'Pastoral' Participation
in the Mass

> That sound tradition may be retained, and yet, the way be
> open for legitimate progress, a careful investigation is always
> to be made into each part of the liturgy which is to be revised.
> This investigation should be . . . pastoral.[1]

I. The Mass: from Jesus to Vatican II

Ever since Jesus Christ took bread and wine at the Last Supper
and, giving them to His disciples, said, *"This is my Body . . .
This is my blood. . . . Do this in memory of me,"* the Roman
Catholic Church has been celebrating the Mass in accordance with
His mandate. The latest chapter in this nearly 2,000-year tradition
was begun in 1969 when Pope Paul VI promulgated the *Roman
Missal,* which had been ordered revised by decree of the Second
Vatican Council. An explanation of how we Catholics celebrate the
Mass today in conformity with this *Missal,* and of why we carry it
out in this precise fashion, is the subject of *A CATHOLIC BOOK OF
THE MASS.*

A. Center of Church's Life and Activity

The Mass doesn't exhaust the entire life and activity of the
Church (cf. SC n. 9). And yet, because the most Blessed Eucharist
"contains the Church's entire spiritual wealth, that is, Christ Himself," present in a way (Real Presence) that surpasses all the other various and rich ways in which He is present to His People (cf.
SC n. 7), and because the Eucharistic Action is the "very heartbeat" (PO n. 5)[2] of the Church, where the "Church reveals herself

Holy Transfiguration Monastery

13

The Monks of Mt. Tabor
(Byzantine-Ukrainian Catholic)

17001 Tomki Rd., Redwood Valley, CA 95470
(707) 485-8959

most clearly" (SC n. 41), the Mass (along with and at the heart of the rest of the Church's liturgy) is at the very center of the Church's life as THE activity of the Church where most powerfully are achieved the "sanctification of men in Christ and the glorification of God" (SC n. 10), and as THE activity "to which all other activities of the Church are directed as toward their goal" (SC n. 10).

This central position of the Mass in the life of the Church has its basis in both belief and practice, and it renders the Mass a portrait in miniature of the whole life of the Church down through the ages. For not only is the Mass the very reenactment in time and space of the saving sacrifice of Jesus on the cross — the *Paschal Mystery* — offered to us by Jesus under the sacramental signs of bread and wine as a meal we share, in promised anticipation of Jesus' Second Coming at the end of time, but the Mass is also in the practical sphere the barometer and nerve center and prism through which all the varying influences of the past 2,000 years — be they people, events or ideas — have had an immediate effect upon the daily life of the faithful, and equally well has provided an open view to the world at large of all that the Church is.

The 2,000 years of Catholics celebrating the Mass do not always read like the measured tones of a catechism or doctrinal tract. Often enough, because of a difference in biblical interpretation or because of historical circumstance or theological controversy, its narration more closely resembles a Sherlock Holmes detective thriller or a Horatio Alger adventure novel. The last twenty years have provided many such moments, since prior to Vatican II the Roman Catholic Mass was being celebrated in essentially the same way that Pope Saint Pius V had established 400 years earlier. As a focal point of belief and practice the Mass was perhaps the single greatest sign of the Church's stability in the face of the Protestant Reformation. Accordingly, these past two decades have been a dream come true for those who had vigorously welcomed the combined efforts of the liturgical movement and of the Church universal which came to fruition in the Second Vatican Council's *Constitution on the Sacred Liturgy*; but they have been a nightmare for others who saw the bulwark of their faith and devotion altered in a matter of a few brief years.

B. 'Radically" reformed by Vatican II

Radical is not an inappropriate label for what Vatican II's liturgical reform accomplished, since it provided "the charter for
the most deliberate and comprehensive remolding of the Church's
worship that has ever taken place,"[3] and it produced this by digging
down to the very roots of the liturgy. Vatican II did not only seek to
preserve "what our immediate ancestors passed on to us"[4] but
rather "the entire past of the Church and all its customs."[5] This requires that not only the Mass according to the *Missal* of Pope Saint
Pius V be "studied profoundly and understood"[6] but also the worship of

> the Christian communities which flourished among the Semit-
> ic, Greek, and Latin peoples [*who*] differed from one another
> in the forms of human and social culture by which they pro-
> fessed one common faith.[7]

Taking this long look at its tradition enabled the Church to view the
Mass from its "broader perspective":[8] "how the Holy Spirit keeps
the people of God faithful in preserving the deposit of faith un-
changed, while prayers and rites differ greatly."[9] Thus at one and
the same time Vatican II "reaffirmed the dogmatic statements of
the Council of Trent,"[10] but in response to the needs of our own
times and on the basis of much liturgical scholarship that has only
taken place during the last two centuries, it has been able "to bring
forward proposals and plans of a pastoral nature which could not
have been foreseen four centuries ago,"[11] and this includes especially "a major step forward in liturgical tradition"[12] — the reform
of the Mass and of the rest of the liturgy.

1. A reform that is both pastoral and traditional

If Vatican II could dare to be radical, it could only do so by
keeping in view both the *pastoral* and *traditional* dimensions of
the Church. The pastoral dimension has not surprisingly received
bigger headlines, but if one looks carefully at the scope of its meaning, stretching from Jesus to the present day, pastoral and traditional are revealed as two sides of the one coin that is the reality of
the Church.

Jesus is the pastor, the Good Shepherd, par excellence (cf.

John 10). This image was a favorite of Vatican II and serves as a model for all Christians. Jesus exercised this role in many and diverse ways, but in none more succinctly than when He criticized the scribes and Pharisees (Mark 7:8): " 'You put aside the commandment of God to cling to human traditions.' " Sometimes, then, a change or development is necessary to recover authentic tradition. The Letter to the Hebrews, in reflecting upon Jesus as High Priest, expresses this same truth when it speaks of Jesus as the faithful servant of God in all things and yet also commpassionate to every need of weak human nature (cf. Hebrews ch. 3, 5). This traditional yet pastoral stance shows itself throughout the history of the Church, whether it be Jesus himself or the early Christians at the "Council of Jerusalem," where, according to Acts 15, the relationship between Judaism and Christianity was definitively settled, or at the Council of Trent, where the attacks of the Reformers were answered, or the *aggiornamento* (Italian for "renewal") of Pope John XXIII, who initiated the reforms of Vatican II.

If the pastoral dimension of the Church's ministry received bigger headlines at and following the time of Vatican II, this is in large part due to *Gaudium et Spes*, Vatican II's Pastoral Constitution on the Church in the Modern World. This major conciliar document not only includes *pastoral* in its title but concretely spells out its meaning in what is by far the lengthiest work of the Council. Its first part is mainly doctrinal in nature, while the second part is pastoral and makes practical applications of the Church's faith to some of the main problems of the day: marriage, family, development of culture, economic, social and political life and peace in the world. *Gaudium et Spes* pledges the Church to uphold human dignity — a gift from God to each person — in every circumstance; it welcomes the advances of human culture and learning; it encourages Christians to become involved in the world; it expresses its desire of dialoguing with the world and of putting itself at the service of the world.[13] In short, *Gaudium et Spes* strikes a note of optimism and openness:

> Let there be unity in what is necessary,
> freedom in what is unsettled,
> and charity in any case.[14]

GS, however, is also deeply steeped in the tradition of the Church. For, despite "significant new emphases and occasional advances in thought or attitude,"[15] GS sets forth "teaching already accepted in the Church" (GS n. 91). The Church thus "guards the heritage of God's Word and draws moral and religious principles without always having at hand the solutions to particular problems" (GS n. 33). *Pastoral*, then, isn't any more synonymous with pragmatic or idyllic than *traditional* is synonymous with blind and unquestioning adherence to the way that things have always been thought or done.

GS marks a major advance in the Church's understanding and statement of its ministry as both pastoral and traditional, and this helps immensely in appreciating the liturgical reform and adaptation carried out by Vatican II. Yet even the pastoral and traditional remain hopelessly at odds unless they are anchored in Jesus, Second Person of the Blessed Trinity, who became like us humans in all things but sin. Accordingly, the Church and every aspect of her life and mission are endowed with both a divine and human element which form nonetheless "one interlocked reality" and which "by an excellent analogy" (LG n. 8)[16] can be "compared to the mystery of the incarnate Word" (LG n. 8). Like her founder, the Church exists in such a way that in her "the human is directed and subordinated to the divine, the visible likewise to the invisible, action to contemplation, and this present world to that city yet to come, which we seek. . ." (SC n. 2).

This means that the Mass we celebrate on earth is a sharing in mystery of that heavenly liturgy where Christ is sitting at the right hand of the Father with all the saints in glory "toward which we journey as pilgrims" (SC n. 8).

This means that we traditionally have one foot planted in the past and the other pastorally planted in the present with an eye on the future. It means that in view of the Incarnation — Jesus taking on our human nature — and of the Resurrection — our human nature being raised to the glory of God — we can never despise what is human. It means that the Church is always in need of reform and nowhere is this more visible than in the liturgy:

> For the liturgy is made up of unchangeable elements divinely instituted, and elements subject to change. The latter not only

may but ought to be changed with the passing of time. . . (SC n. 21).

Reform and adaptation are required and carried out in conformity with the nature of the liturgy and in response to the pastoral needs of the times.

The work and spirit of the Council of Trent are often contrasted unfavorably with that of Vatican II. Yet what unites the two of them is much more fundamental than what divides them. The wisest members of the Church, whether in A.D. 85 or A.D. 1985, have always recognized this. Two great English Catholics nurtured by the work and spirit of Trent have each expressed this in their own unique ways. In his work on the development of Christian doctrine Cardinal Newman wrote: "In a higher world it is otherwise; but here below to live is to change, and to be perfect is to have changed often."[17] G.K. Chesterton, the noted journalist and author, put the same truth in more concrete terms:

> All conservatism goes upon the assumption that if you leave a thing alone, you leave a thing as it is. But you do not. If you leave a thing to itself, you are leaving it to wild and violent changes. All nature is change. . . . For instance, if you want a white house . . . and leave it white in our atmosphere, it will soon be black. If you want a white house, you must be continually painting it white, beginning all over again and re-creating your ideal. In other words, if you want your old white house, you must have a new white house. You must have a revolution. . . . The foundation of the true doctrine of progress is that all things tend to get worse. Man must perpetually interfere to resist a natural degeneration; if man does not reform a thing, Nature will deform it. He must always be altering the thing even in order to keep it the same. If a man wants to keep his garden the same, he does not leave it to itself, for left to itself it will become quite different. If he wants it to remain the same, he goes about it with a ferocious speed, uprooting things like a walking revolution. For the man who weeds plays the part of a pitiless and positive uprooter. In other words, he plays the part of a Radical. The trimness and tidiness of all our gardens depends upon a persistent Radicalism; and all those ranked flowers and rigid lawns are kept clear and quiet by a principle of perpetual revolution. Similarly, every spring cleaning is a revolution but, like all others, a conservative revolution. Like all other revolutions, it disturbs, maddens, de-

stroys and may even degrade. But its object is to give a man
his old clean house. . . . The white house must be washed and
painted at the first hint of grey.[18]

Both Newman and Chesterton penned their words before entering
the Roman Catholic Church.

If *pastoral* is the word and attitude most often associated with
Vatican II,

> In the restoration and promotion of the sacred liturgy . . . it
> is full and active participation by all the people which is the
> aim to be considered before all else; for it is the primary and
> indispensable source from which the faithful are to derive the
> true Christian spirit (SC n. 14).

This vision of full community participation hearkens back to the
classical age of the Mass before the sixth century when the
"Church appears to have been spontaneous and without problems
in her community celebration of the Eucharist"[19] (cf. SC n. 41), and
before a later time when the Mass progressively became the function of the clergy and the rest of the faithful remained devoutly
present in silence (cf. SC n. 48).

2. Full participation: keystone of the reform

The basis of this communal participation is not a democratic
notion of the Twentieth Century graciously accorded to the people;
it is demanded by the "very nature of the liturgy" (SC n. 14). It is
the "right and duty" (SC n. 14) of the Christian people by reason of
Baptism, which constitutes us a " 'chosen race, a royal priesthood,
a holy nation, a purchased people' " (1 Peter 2:9; cf. 2:4-5). The
Mass that the Church offers is the Priestly Prayer of Jesus Christ,
and it is only by virtue of His priesthood that the Christian People,
whether through Baptism or Holy Orders, are able to participate in
the Mass. And, this participation in the Mass is the high point of
participation in God's Plan of Salvation which has as its aim "to
dignify men with a participation in His own divine life" (LG n. 2).
Even after man and woman sinned, God re-created us in Christ and
sent the Holy Spirit on Pentecost to give life to the Church Christ
had founded.

God's offer of salvation to us is not intended as a monologue on

God's part. God issues an invitation and He expects a reply. The
Mass, then — like the whole life of Faith — is a dialogue between
God and His People. Participation at the Mass is a total involvement: every Catholic fully present throughout the entire Mass and
committed to completing all that leads up to the Mass and all that
should result from it. Attendance at Mass involves an active participation in both the Liturgy of the Word and the Liturgy of the Eucharist, the two main and inseparable parts of the Mass. This participation is both external and internal (cf. SC n. 19): it demands
not only the commitment of one's body to carry out the ritual, but
the total commitment of mind and heart as well. Each Catholic
must properly prepare himself to celebrate the Mass by cultivating
a personal prayer life and by observing "all that Christ has commanded. . ." (SC n. 9). Mass in reality neither begins nor ends
within the walls of the Church. Thus, participation at Mass spills
over into everyday life, as St. John Chrysostom witnesses:

> Do you want to honor Christ's body? Then do not scorn Him
> in His nakedness, nor honor Him here in the church with silken
> garments while neglecting him outside where he is cold and na-
> ked. For He who said, *This is my body*, and made it so by his
> words, also said: *You saw me hungry and did not feed me*,
> and *inasmuch as you did not do it for one of these, the
> least of my brothers, you did not do it for me*. What we do
> here in the church requires a pure heart, not special garments;
> what we do outside requires great dedication.[20]

The Mass is not just a way of worshiping but a way of living.
   To "participate knowingly, devoutly, and actively" (SC n. 48)
at Mass is a major part of what constitutes our life of faith in the
Church: to be "instructed by God's Word" and "be refreshed at the
table of the Lord's body"; to "give thanks to God . . . by offering
the Immaculate Victim, not only through the hands of the priest,
but also with him; and "to offer" ourselves as well and to do all of
this so that "Through Christ the Mediator, . . . all will be drawn
day by day into ever closer union with God and with each other, so
that finally God may be all in all" (SC n. 48).
   To achieve this full and productive participation it is first necessary to have a "proper appreciation of the rites and prayers" of
the Mass. (SC n. 48), and this effort has a number of dimensions. It

is nothing less than being familiar with the whole process that Vatican II followed in reforming the Mass:

> That sound tradition may be retained, and yet the way be open for legitimate progress, a careful investigation is always to be made into each part of the liturgy which is to be revised (SC n. 23).

And this investigation must be scriptural, historical, theological and liturgical in nature (cf. SC n. 23-24). This provides both the ideal of full participation in the Mass and the framework of *A CATHOLIC BOOK OF THE MASS*: a basic familiarity with the two basic parts of the Mass — the Liturgy of the Word (Chapter Six) and the Liturgy of the Eucharist (Chapter Seven) and with its scriptural (Chapter Two), historical (Chapter Three), theological (Chapter Four) and liturgical (Chapter Five) foundations.

Although the aim of *A CATHOLIC BOOK OF THE MASS* is a better understanding of the 2,000-year tradition of the Mass, and thus, it is hoped, a better celebration of it, the Mass, because it is a mystery of Faith, can never be fully captured by human thought or language. This shouldn't discourage our efforts but rather encourage us all the more to deepen our knowledge and thus our love of the Mass. Pope Paul VI directed us in this way when he defined mystery as a "reality imbued with the hidden presence of God. It lies, therefore . . . always open to new and greater exploration."[21] Concretely this is evidenced for the Mass by the variety of names by which it has been known throughout history. Often they are used interchangeably, but each has a more or less precise meaning which underlines a dimension of the Mass that the others do not.

In the earliest accounts of the Mass St. Paul speaks of it as the *Lord's Supper* (I Corinthians 11). St. Luke, in both the Gospel of Luke and the Acts of the Apostles, speaks of the *Breaking of the Bread. Eucharist* is the term frequently used in the period following the death of the Twelve Apostles. It means "giving thanks" and is related to the Jewish Passover meal's blessing and thanksgiving over the several cups of wine drunk during the course of the Passover meal. In the New Testament it comes to refer to the whole of the New Passover celebrated by Jesus for the first time at the Last Supper. *Sacrifice* is early applied to the Mass because of its intimate connection with Christ's death on the hill of Calvary

Liturgy is the preferred term for the Mass in the Eastern Church, while in the Western Church this term has a more comprehensive meaning: "in the liturgy full public worship is performed by the Mystical Body of Jesus Christ, that is, by the Head and His members" (SC n. 7). Thus, Vatican II's Constitution on the Sacred Liturgy treats the whole liturgy of the Church: the Mass and the other six sacraments, sacramentals, the Liturgy of the Hours, the Liturgical Year and sacred music, art and furnishings.

Beginning in the fifth century, the term *Mass* emerged as standard usage for the celebration of the Eucharist in the Western Church — more specifically, in the Roman Rite. Like the term *Eucharist*, this term originally applied only to a certain part of the celebration: to the dismissal (in Latin: *Ite, missa est*) when it was customary to impart a blessing to those in attendance and the Mass accordingly was so understood as God's preeminent blessing.

Whether we prefer *Mass* or *Eucharist* or *Liturgy* or any one of the countless other names that have emerged through the centuries, their variety is a reminder that no one of them expresses the totality of this Mystery and so no one of them can be forgotten.

C. 'Pastoral' Participation in the Mass

Chapter One of *A CATHOLIC BOOK OF THE MASS* is basically an introduction to an introduction to the Mass. It sought to explain why Pope Paul VI spoke of the liturgy as the "first subject to be examined by Vatican II and the first, too, in a sense, in intrinsic worth and in importance for the life of the Church."[22] With no hesitation, it responded to this by tracing the Mass's centrality to what Jesus said and did at the Last Supper, and in the latest chapter of this nearly 2,000-year tradition initiated by Vatican II, it spoke of the Church's efforts to return the Mass to the "best of liturgical tradition."[23] It highlighted Vatican II's pastoral sensitivity in first addressing itself to the liturgy, where the majority of Catholics would most quickly benefit from the conciliar reforms, but in doing this Vatican II was only continuing to do what the Church has always sought to do: to faithfully fulfill "its responsibility as the teacher of truth to guard the 'old,' that is, the deposit of tradition"[24] and at the same time to fulfill "another responsibility, that of examining and prudently introducing the 'new.' "[25]

Full participation by all the faithful in the liturgy was the keystone of Vatican II's liturgical renewal, and Chapter One has attempted to underscore that this participation has many dimensions. And if there is any one dimension that it has stressed, it is that Catholics must always keep in view the entirety of their long and rich tradition of belief in and celebration of the Mass. This involves keeping the "broader perspective" of which Pope Paul VI spoke and not viewing any period — either in positive or negative terms — in isolation from the rest of the tradition or divorced from its historical background. This kind of short-sightedness is like looking at a beautiful flower and not taking into account the plant that produced it or the roots that nourished it. In keeping this full vision before him, the Catholic can appreciate the vast plan of God for man's salvation in which the Mass plays so pivotal a part, a plan in which we are all called to participate by God in a personal way through the Church. Then we can more easily understand how the divine and the human, how the pastoral and the traditional, how continuity and change intertwine and render "new" and "old" very relative terms in the vocabulary of the faith of the Church. Thus, by following the letter and the spirit of Vatican II's liturgical renewal, our participation in the Mass will resemble " *'the scribe who becomes a disciple of the kingdom of heaven and is like a householder who brings out from his storeroom things both new and old'* " (Matthew 13:52).

Chapter One: Discussion Questions

1. Discuss how the Mass is the doctrinal and practical nerve-center of the Church and how this is reflected in your own parish community.

2. Discuss the effect of the last twenty years on your parish. Chart the high and low points of that period. You might do the same for your own personal relationship with the Mass; e.g., did you welcome the reforms of Vatican II, oppose them, change your opinion concerning them?

3. Discuss and define the word pastoral in reference to the liturgy. Is the liturgy the center of pastoral activity in your parish?

4. Do you think that most Catholics tend more readily to contrast the Councils of Trent and Vatican II than to compare them? Do some further

research on the pastoral response of the Council of Trent to the needs of its time. Are there any lessons there for today?

5. What implications does *Gaudium et Spes* have for the parish Sunday liturgy? For instance, are the main issues of *GS* brought up: the family, peace, etc.?

6. Discuss some of the difficulties in distinguishing between Tradition and traditions.

7. Discuss the difference between merely external change and the internal change that should underlie all active participation in the liturgy.

8. How does each of the names for the Mass point to a common underlying reality and yet emphasize one particular aspect of the reality that is the Eucharist?

CHAPTER TWO

'Scriptural' Participation in the Mass

Sacred Scripture is of paramount importance in the celebration of the liturgy . . . and if the restoration, progress, and adaptation of the sacred liturgy are to be achieved, it is necessary to promote . . . a warm and living love for Scripture (SC n. 24).

II. Sacred Scripture: the Eucharist and Jesus Christ

This is my body and *This is my blood* are probably the words of Jesus that Catholics most often speak and hear spoken in church. This is not inappropriate, since by these words Jesus "summarized orally and ritually the whole mystery"[1] of His life: "He recalled his coming in the flesh in Mary's womb; He anticipated His death by adding 'given for you'; He announced His resurrection by which He would be able to continue the gift of himself"[2] by adding *Do this in memory of me.* In a word, Jesus instituted the Eucharist.

A. Sacred Scripture: the Origin of the Eucharist

The Bible is the first chapter of any book on the Mass. The very first lines of the Liturgy Constitution's chapter on the Mass focus our attention on this scriptural dimension of the Eucharist which is the main concern of this Chapter Two: "At the Last Supper, on the night when He was betrayed, our Savior instituted the Eucharistic Sacrifice of His Body and Blood" (SC n. 47). This scriptural basis of the Mass will be investigated in the four Gospels and St. Paul, but a necessary prelude to this is to situate these key biblical texts

not only in the wider context of Vatican II but also in that of Divine
Revelation itself.

1. Scripture and Vatican II

The Second Vatican Council is markedly scriptural in its out-
look and spirit, terminology and images. The *Constitution on
Divine Revelation* expresses the reason for this in terms of the
Mass:

> The Church has always venerated the divine Scriptures just
> as she venerates the body of the Lord, since from the table of
> both the word of God and of the body of Christ she unceasingly
> receives and offers to the faithful the bread of life, especially
> in the sacred liturgy (DV n. 21).[3]

Concretely, then, many results issued from the Council's wish that
"easy access to sacred Scripture should be provided for all the
Christian faithful" (DV n. 22): a more abundant and diverse use of
Scripture, especially at Mass, a biblically based homily, use of the
vernacular and Scripture services, to mention only a few.

2. Scripture and the contemporary biblical movement

This renewal in biblical studies that came to fruition at the
Council had a long preparation. From the Council of Trent in the
16th century until the mid-19th century, Catholic biblical works
were marked by a strongly apologetic response to the various Protestant attacks on Catholic belief and practice regarding Scripture
and Tradition, especially concerning the Mass. The mid-1800s witnessed the publication of works of a more learned and scientific nature and this has resulted in the steady appearance of many fine
Catholic biblical scholars and the establishment of centers and as-
sociations and publications devoted to Catholic biblical studies.
This renewal was especially aided by Pope Leo XIII and his encyclical letter *Providentissimus Deus* (1893), by Pope Benedict
XV and his *Spiritus Paraclitus* (1920) and especially by Pope
Pius XII's *Divino Afflante Spiritu* (1943).

3. Scripture and Divine Revelation

Even more important, however, is it necessary to understand
the relationship between Scripture and the Mass in terms of Divine

Revelation, which simply put is the Word of God, "the power of God for the salvation of all who believe" (DV n. 17). Out of His infinite love God has revealed Himself to His People that we might share His life and love on earth and then one day in fullness in His Kingdom. God accomplishes this through the gift of His creation, especially through that of man and woman, whom He made in His own image and likeness, but most fully in the gift to humanity (the Incarnation) of His Son, who consummated this marriage of God with man by His supreme act of love on the cross. This is the Person and event and message the Church continues to proclaim by the power of the Holy Spirit, whom the Risen Savior conferred upon it at Pentecost.

Divine Revelation reaches its high point in Jesus, the Word of God (cf. Hebrews 1:1-4), who founded the Church to continue His mission on earth, and He endowed it with all the gifts necessary to carry out this mandate. Thus Divine Revelation in its fullness involves Sacred Scripture, Sacred Tradition and the Magisterium, the teaching office of the Church. Sacred Scripture is the Word of God inasmuch as it is consigned to writing under the inspiration of the Holy Spirit. (DV n. 9). This includes both Old Testament and New Testament: "God, the inspirer and author of both testaments, wisely arranged that the New Testament be hidden in the Old and the Old be made manifest in the New" (DV n. 16). The Gospels are the principal witnesses of the life and teaching of Jesus and they tell us "the honest truth about Jesus" (DV n. 19).

The Church, however, doesn't "draw her certainty about everything which has been revealed" (DV n. 9) from Scripture alone. Although from after the death of the last of the Twelve Apostles the Church has awaited no "further new public revelation before the glorious manifestation of our Lord Jesus Christ" (DV n. 4), it is the Church's mission under the guidance of the Holy Spirit to faithfully live and hand on the Word of God in all its purity through the ages and "to grow in it, to nourish its development, and to make it living and effective, a leaven to renew the earth."[4] We can even say

that revelation continues in the sense that the living God remains present to His people, and by His continuing care and His gifts of graces enables them to recognize and love Him and the good news of the Gospel.[5]

This Sacred Tradition flows from the "same divine wellspring" as Sacred Scripture (DV n. 9), and both "merge into a unity and tend toward the same end" (DV n. 9). In fact, it is through this "same tradition" (DV n. 8) that the very books of the Bible became known and are ever more deeply understood and made active in the Church.

This Sacred Tradition is the living and active presence of God in His Church. It is God continually conversing with the Church, the bride of His Son, and through her with the world in the power of the Holy Spirit. This action of God elicits the response of men and women professing and practicing their Faith and this living and lived tradition of the Faith develops in the Church with the help of the Holy Spirit through the contemplation and study of believers, through their understanding of what they experience and especially through the ministry of preaching exercised in the Church (cf. DV n. 8), and this will continue through the ages, as "the Church constantly moves forward toward the fullness of divine truth when the words of God reach their complete fulfillment in her" (DV n. 8).

The Church believes that "God has seen to it that what He had revealed for the salvation of all nations would abide perpetually in its full integrity and be handed on to all generations" (DV n. 7). Accordingly, although it serves the Word of God and is not above it, the "living teaching office of the Church" (DV n. 10) has been entrusted with the special task of "authentically interpreting the Word of God, whether written or handed on" (DV n. 10). In this way the "supreme rule of faith" (DV n. 21) — Sacred Scripture and Sacred Tradition, along with the Church's teaching office — are so joined together that one can't stand without the others and "all together and each in its own way under the action of the one Holy Spirit contribute effectively to the salvation of souls" (DV n. 10).

Against this background of Vatican II and the whole of Divine Revelation, the liturgy's intimate relationship with Scripture and Tradition can better be understood and appreciated. For it shows that the words of institution which Jesus pronounced over the bread and wine were recounted at the celebration of the Mass before they came to be written down in the books of the Bible. The liturgy was actually an aid in preserving, formulating and handing on some of the most essential parts of Scripture. This is also true for such Old Testament works as the Book of Psalms, a vital part of both Old and New Testament worship. Thus Divine Revelation emerges as a living reality, a personal encounter with the Word of God from generation to generation, and there is no more privileged moment for that than in the Mass and the rest of the liturgy.

B. The Institution Narratives

The words of institution of the Eucharist neither exhaust the richness of Divine Revelation nor even that of the Mass itself; yet they enjoy a prime position in both. Taken as a unity, the accounts present a vision of the Church's scripturally based belief in and celebration of the Eucharist, and taken individually, they evidence the wealth of variety that characterizes the Church's 2,000-year Eucharistic tradition.

1. Matthew 26:26-29 and Mark 14:22-25

Because of their extensive agreement, which can be easily displayed in parallel columns, the Gospels of Mark, Matthew and Luke are called "synoptic." This is especially visible in their accounts of the Last Supper, varying considerably from that of the Gospel of John, which reports no words of institution over the bread and wine.

Of the synoptic Gospels, Mark and Matthew bear special comparison: 1) the common origin of their accounts of the Last Supper is the Church in Palestine; 2) a clear parallelism between the elements of bread and wine is manifested: *This is my body. . . . This is my blood*; 3) the aspect of blood is given a special emphasis: For *this is my blood of the covenant*; 4) the sacrificial aspect of Jesus' death is emphasized, centering upon the cup: *Which is to be poured out for many for the forgiveness of sins* (only Matthew adds *for the forgiveness of sins*); 5) the cup is also stressed as the symbol of the joy of the Kingdom to come, "a toast to the future":[6] *I tell you I shall not drink again of this fruit of the vine until that day when I drink it new with you in my Father's kingdom*, and 6) notably absent is *Do this in memory of me*.

By way of contrast, Matthew adds an emphatic *Eat* and *Drink* and *for the forgiveness of sins*. Mark 1:15 presents John the Baptist proclaiming a baptism of repentance for the forgiveness of sins; Matthew saves this for the critical moment of the institution of the Eucharist. By contrast with the other three Gospels, the style of Mark is concise and economical.

2. Luke 22:14-20; 24:13-35; Acts 2:13-21; 42-47; 20:7-12

In addition to its similarities with the other synoptic Gospels, Matthew and Mark, Luke's account of the Last Supper — unlike that of Matthew and Mark — gives great prominence to the farewell discourses of Jesus, an element it shares with the account of John. Luke also bears a number of similarities to the account of Paul. These both have their origin in the Church at Antioch; they include *Do this in memory of me.* Luke records this after the blessing of the bread, while Paul does after the blessing of the cup. Luke puts emphasis on bread by speaking of the Eucharist as *breaking of the bread.* Yet, curiously enough, the element of wine is also emphasized, for in some manuscripts of Luke, Jesus blesses the cup twice — an interesting touch from the pagan-born author of Luke who retains — unlike the Jewish Mark, Matthew and John — more of the Last Supper's original Passover-meal structure, which contained multiple blessings of the cup. As in Matthew and Mark, the cup has a strong eschatological significance in the Last Supper account of Luke, but in his other work, Acts, part of this future joy has already been realized in the new Church. In Acts 2:13-21, Peter responds to the charge that he and his companions have drunk *too much new wine* by quoting the words of the Prophet Joel (3:1): *I [God] will pour out a portion of my spirit on all mankind.* The new wine of the Kingdom is the joy of new life in the Holy Spirit.

Both Luke and Acts witness to the basic twofold structure of the Mass: the Liturgy of the Word and the Liturgy of the Eucharist. Luke's account of the Emmaus episode — on the day of the Resurrection — refers to these two elements and to the dynamic movement which flows through them to a climax in the "breaking of the bread." Cleopas and another disciple of Jesus recount to the unrecognized, risen Savior the "bad news" of Calvary and the dashing of their hopes of a messiah. Jesus gives them the "good news" of how the Old Testament foretold this and actually prepared for the coming of Jesus and His salvific death on the cross and His resurrection. Yet only after Jesus blessed, broke, and distributed the bread were the eyes of the disciples opened to recognize Jesus and the full meaning of the words of Scripture: *Were not our hearts burning inside us as he talked to us on the road and explained the scriptures to us?* The Person of Jesus, THE Word of God — and the words of Sacred Scripture — are only understood in fullness in the context of the two-part unity which is the Mass.

Acts 2:46 witnesses to this same basic structure: *They* [the early Christians] *went as a body to the temple every day but met in their houses for the breaking of the bread.* The early Christians felt quite comfortable in joining the Jews in the temple or synagogue for the Sabbath scripture and prayer liturgy — a service such as Jesus attends in Luke 4:16ff., which is basically (with the addition of the New Testament readings) the Liturgy of the Word — and then retired to their homes for the Liturgy of the Eucharist.

3. John 13-17; John 6

The Gospel of John varies in many notable ways from those of Matthew, Mark and Luke, and this is no more evident than in the account of the Last Supper. There are points of similarity with all three of them, but the differences are striking: 1) the very length of the account; 2) the meaning of the account, treated at length; 3) the absence of a preparation for the meal; 4) the absence of Jesus' words of institution over the bread and wine; 5) the addition of the washing of the feet of the disciples, and 6) a long, last discourse of Jesus. A seventh notable difference from the synoptics is the matter of dating the Passover and the Crucifixion. John dates these events one day earlier than do the synoptics. In this way John pictures Jesus' condemnation and death at the time when the priests began to slaughter the paschal lambs in the Temple area. The Last Supper in John retains its crucial connection with the Passover feast, although Jesus had already been laid in the tomb when the Jews began the Passover Supper. For Matthew, Mark and Luke the Last Supper and the events of the Passion span the feast of Passover: from sundown Thursday to sundown Friday. The reasons for this chronological divergence are much disputed.

There are many possible interpretations for the meaning of the foot washing: an example of humility or a reference to the sacraments of Baptism and the Eucharist.[7] But, it is clear that this action touches the very core of the meaning of Jesus' whole life and ministry as well as of this particular event of the Last Supper: *If I do not wash you, you can have nothing in common with me.* Jesus startled His disciples by doing an action normally done by servants, but this novel behavior was part of the first fruits of the *new commandment*, the cornerstone of the new era He was now beginning: *Just as I have loved you, you also must love one another* (13:34) and *A man can have no greater love than to lay down his life for his friends* (15:13). This belief and practice are what constitute a disciple.

Jesus bids the disciples farewell at the Last Supper but gives them hope by telling them that He goes to prepare a place for them, where they will eventually be able to join Him. In the meantime He assures them of His continued presence with them as they witness to Him in the world, and that they *will perform the same works as I do myself . . .* and *even greater works.* This will come about because Jesus will send the *Advocate* or *Paraclete* in His place from the Father. This *Advocate*, the Holy Spirit, is the answer to Jesus' Priestly Prayer in chapter 17 of John. In this way the disciples will be unified in a way that can be broken by neither the Prince of this world, nor by hatred of this world, nor by persecution, expulsion from the Temple, being scattered, or even by death itself. Nothing can break this community of life and love between Jesus and the disciples, which is a very sharing in the life and love of the Trinity: *May they all be one: may they be one in us, as you, Father, are in me and I am in you, so that the world may believe it was you who sent me.*

Although our understanding and appreciation of the Last Supper are immeasurably enriched by inclusion of the foot washing and the lengthy discourses, John's omission of the words of institution raises many questions and has given rise to many theories to account for it. Of these, one solution is to turn to John 6, the Discourse on the Bread of Life. Raymond Brown advances the theory that

> the backbone of verses 51-58 is made up of material from the Johannine narrative of the institution of the Eucharist, which originally was located in the Last Supper scene and that this material has been recast into a duplicate of the Bread of Life Discourse.[8]

Brown also notes that Chapter 13 shows the marks of this deletion.[9]

Brown bases this theory on a number of points. The language of verse 51 is very similar to that of the institution narratives found in the synoptics and Paul:[10]

> I am the living bread that has come down from heaven.
> Anyone who eats this bread will live forever;
> and the bread that I shall give
> is my flesh, for the life of the world.

John 6 opens with the story of the multiplication of the loaves, the only miracle story to occur in all four of the Gospels, and it has a strong Eucharistic tone in all of them. As do Matthew and Mark, John includes here as well the episode of Jesus walking on the water, which suggests the Passover theme of God leading His people safely through the Red Sea, and its importance is emphasized by John's placing it between the multiplication of the loaves and the Bread of Life discourse. Finally, the language of John throughout the Gospel is very sacramental and symbolic — e.g., use of water, fire, light, bread, among others — although the precise nature of this is much discussed.

It is also possible to see in John 6:35-58 "the structural skeleton"[11] of the Mass, Liturgy of the Word and Liturgy of the Eucharist. Verses 35-50 sound the wisdom theme of complete adherence to the Word of God: *it is not to do my own will that I have come down from heaven, but to do the will of him who sent me.* Verses 51-58 have the Eucharist as their main theme. John changes the vocabulary from the previous verses and now we hear: *eat, drink, flesh, blood.* This is then reinforced by references to the Old Testament manna God gave to His People in the desert and to the theme of Passover. Also — like Paul — John uses the more graphic term *flesh* — rather than *body*, which the synoptics use — and since there is a word in Hebrew and Aramaic for *flesh* but not for *body*, the language of John and Paul might well be closer to the language of Jesus. In general, then — just as we saw in Luke — these two parts of the Bread of Life discourse represent the twofold presence of Jesus to the faithful: in the "preached word"[12] and in the "sacrament of the Eucharist."[13] So it is that, while the synoptics and Paul record the actual words of institution, John explains their meaning at length, and if we look to an earlier chapter of John (6) we see evidence of what might have been his own version of the words of institution set in a passage that further explains the meaning of the Eucharist and gives witness to the twofold structure of the Mass.

4. 1 Corinthians 11:17-34; 1 Corinthians 10

The similarities between Paul and Luke have already been discussed; by contrast, the Corinthian community, which Paul takes to task, is far different from the Jerusalem Church that Acts evidences:

> *All lived together and owned everything in common; they sold their goods and possessions and shared out the proceeds among themselves according to what each one needed* (Acts 2:44-45).

In 1 Corinthians 11, Paul — using his authority as an apostle — addresses a community where certain members have actually excommunicated and condemned themselves by breaking into factions at the Lord's Supper and its accompanying common meal. Earlier, in 1 Corinthians 10, he had warned Christians that participation in sexual immorality and pagan sacrificial meals keeps the Christian from a worthy participation in the Eucharist.

These acute pastoral problems provide Paul the occasion to expound upon the meaning of the words and actions of Jesus at the Last Supper, which demand as well the spirit and attitude of Jesus to make of them a worthy memorial of the Lord's Supper. For, the Corinthians' behavior is not merely a breach of good manners. To participate worthily involves recollecting oneself and realizing that the Lord's Supper is not a matter of ordinary eating and drinking. It is rather, as Paul makes very clear, a sharing in the Body and Blood of Jesus. This Real Presence of Jesus to His People demands in response a total presence of Christians to God and to one another. Thus Paul's emphasis upon the realism of the sacrament of the Eucharist goes hand in hand with the realism of "Love your neighbor." Both the Old and New Testaments are full of invective for those people who perform perfectly the rituals of worship but are blind to carrying out the spirit. Paul insists on the spirit and attitudes of Jesus Himself toward what he calls the Body of Christ (one's fellow Christians) and indeed toward all men and women who are invited to be part of the Church, the Body of Christ.

Paul's language in these passages might sound puritanical, based on fear, even superstitious; but no! In Paul's characteristically forthright manner, he is reminding a beloved community that as often as they eat and drink the Body and Blood of the Lord they are proclaiming His death until He comes again. In other words, even now Jesus, who is sitting in glory at the right hand of the Father, is re-fashioning our human bodies into the image of His own glorified Risen Person. This is accomplished preeminently in the Mass, the celebration of the Lord's death and resurrection, and this not only puts us into a completely new relationship with God but puts our every other relationship as well — with others, the world, ourselves — into a completely new perspective. Since Jesus assumed our human nature, put sin to death in it and raised it to a new level of living and loving, there is no ground where our Christian Faith allows us to remain neutral.

C. Themes that emerge from the Institution Narratives

To complete the treatment of the accounts of institution, it is helpful to consider the significance of: 1) the elements of bread and wine as natural and supernatural symbols; 2) the meal in the time of Jesus; 3) the connection between the Eucharist and the Passover meal and 4) the connection between the Eucharist and the rest of the life of Jesus.

1. The significance of bread and wine

Because bread and wine are elements rich in natural and supernatural significance, Jesus chose them to be the most intimate vehicles of His presence and action in the world. On the natural level, bread and wine were among the chief staples of the diet of Jesus' contemporaries. Also, they have a basic human meaning: bread as the staff of life and wine as the joy of life. They are often seen in the Old Testament: Melchizedek used them in his blessing on Abraham's behalf (Genesis 14:19). They are part of God's blessings to be found in the Promised Land (Deuteronomy 11:14;28:5; 32:14). Ultimately their significance will only be realized in God's kingdom, as Isaiah attests: there all will be invited to come and eat and drink freely and to complete satisfaction (e.g., 62:9; 65:13). They are important elements in Jewish liturgical life: the presentation bread associated with the Ark of the Covenant and the Temple (Exodus 25:30; Leviticus 24:5-9; 1 Samuel 21:4-7). The Feast of Unleavened Bread was the occasion for offering to God the first-fruits of the land. Libations of wine were sprinkled on the front of the altar (Sirach 50:15-17). The cup conjures up the image of God's wrath (Jeremiah 10:25; Ps. 69), as well as conveying a sign of favor — e.g., when the king or high official honored a person by extending his own cup to him. In the Passover meal both bread and wine were important elements. In the New Testament, Jesus refers to Himself as the *bread come down from heaven* (John 6:41) and as the *bread of life* (John 6:35). Significantly, the only miracle found in all four Gospels is that of the multiplication of the loaves. Jesus makes reference to the cup as a symbol of His suffering (especially in the Garden of Gethsemane), a cup which His disciples must share (Matthew 20:22-23; Mark 10:38-39). He also used it as a sign of joy and happiness; e.g., at the wedding feast of Cana when he turned the water into wine (John 2).

2. The significance of the meal

The meal in which the bread and wine are consumed also has a special significance. Although it might be difficult for Americans who have a penchant for "fast" food to imagine, there is no such thing in the East as an ordinary meal. Its comprehensive role as a biological, social and religious focal point of daily life lies behind the practice of the common meal associated with the Eucharist in Paul's account of the institution of the Eucharist. In the meal the physical process of the body's assimilation of food is a sign of the union in friendship and love which binds men and women together to one another and to God in the very act of eating. The meal is an activity, an encounter, which engages a person on every level of human existence. The Eucharist does not blot out the meal's human and cultural meaning, a capacity endowed by the Creator, but brings it to full potential.[14]

Jesus is often pictured eating with various groups in the Gospel. There was, however, no more special meal than the Last Supper, and this was eaten at the holiest time of the Jewish year: the Feast of Passover. Although only certain details in this meal have come down to us, they have provided the basic framework of the Eucharist: Jesus took bread and wine (offertory), blessed it (consecration), broke it and gave it to His disciples (communion). The Jewish sabbath scripture and prayer liturgy was eventually added to this and completes the Mass as we know it. In John, Jesus is called the Lamb of God (recall above how the chronology of John emphasizes this connection in his account of the Passion), but the significance of the paschal lamb was taken over by the element of bread in the Christian Passover. Yet the Passover prayer of blessing and thanksgiving over the cup has given us the term *Eucharist.*

3. Connection between the Eucharist and the Passover meal

Although Jesus' life and ministry encompass more than the Last Supper, the Last Supper, eaten against the background of the Feast of Passover, provides the vehicle by which we can see most clearly the relationship between the Eucharist and the Passion of Jesus, which — with its completion in the Resurrection, the Paschal Mystery — is the crowning point of Jesus' messianic mission. From the historical point of view, the Passion accounts in the Gospels follow immediately upon the Last Supper. From the literary point of view, the Last Supper accounts are filled with references to Jesus' approaching passion and death. And theologically, Jesus gives the meal its ultimate meaning when He delivers up to Calvary the Body and Blood that He has just shared with His disciples at the Last Supper.[15] So just as the Feast of Passover sums up the entire Old Testament, so now in Jesus the Passover is elevated to a new level as it is reenacted in the very Person of Jesus. Taking place at one moment in time and space but extending to every moment in time and space, because it is the eternal, almighty God who is present and active, the Passover is celebrated by Jesus as it never was or could be again: at this one special moment the covenant and promises made through Abraham, Isaac and Jacob, the deliverance of the Hebrews from Egypt, the covenant and promises made through Moses and those foretold by the prophets all reach their fulfillment: *He . . . has offered one single sacrifice for sins. . . . He has achieved the eternal perfection of all whom he is sanctifying* (Hebrews 10:12-14).

4. Connection between the Eucharist and the whole life of Jesus

If the meaning of the Mass is concentrated in the events of the Last Supper, passion, death and resurrection of Jesus, it is of a piece with the rest of His life. Jesus' presence and activity in the Eucharist are anticipated in such as Matthew 1:23, where He is called Emmanuel, "God-with-us," and its special manner is anticipated by the many meals Jesus attended which were the occasions for both teaching people and reconciling them to God. To give further examples is only to repeat the whole of the Gospels.

D. "Scriptural" participation in the Mass

This presentation doesn't exhaust the richness of the relationship between the Mass and Sacred Scripture, but it does give some indication that the Catholic belief in and celebration of the Mass is founded upon the Bible.

I recall reading in a newspaper some years ago about a Protestant clergyman who was lamenting the fact that his flock was woefully unfamiliar with the Bible, so much that he found it difficult to use scriptural language in his homilies. This indeed would be a cause for grave concern among Protestants, who have traditionally been famed for their devotion to and knowledge of Scripture. The Catholic Church at Vatican II also noted that its own faithful were not as familiar with Scripture as should have been the case. Thus, in light of Vatican II's reforms, which directed that Scripture be made more available to the faithful, full participation at Mass involves not only a fuller participation at the Liturgy of the Word, the much-revised first part of the Mass, but also a knowledge of and participation in the whole of the intimate relationship that unites the Mass and Sacred Scripture.

This full participation involves, first off, an understanding and appreciation of the renewal of Vatican II in the area of Scripture: how and why it came about, and how and why this differs from Trent's renewal.

This full participation also involves an understanding and appreciation of the accounts of the Gospels, St. Paul and related writings, which tell us about Jesus' institution of the Eucharist and the early Church's belief in and celebration of the Mass; of the antiquity of the accounts; of their Semitic character, which reflects the world in which Jesus lived; of how they vary in detail of wording and point of view but share a basic structure and meaning which we believe come directly from Jesus; of how the Last Supper is a crucial part of the Gospels and has a special relationship to every part of the Gospels; of how Jesus willingly and confidently celebrated the Last Supper to its completion on the cross and assured His disciples that they would witness and share in its fruits when the Holy Spirit would come to continue His salvific mission on earth, especially the essential role of transforming the bread and wine at Mass into Christ's Body and Blood, His Church's chief nourishment until He comes again.[16]

Full participation involves an understanding and appreciation of how the Church views Scripture — both the Old and New Testament — not in isolation but as a unity with Sacred Tradition and with the Magisterium of the Church. All three of these constitute Divine Revelation, which is conveyed by human words — both written and spoken — but which is *God's word* and not *man's word* (cf. 1 Thess. 2:13) and *which is able to give you the wisdom that leads to salvation through faith in Christ Jesus* (cf. 2 Thess. 2:15). This power for salvation is preserved fully by the Church alone for *there is no prophecy contained in Scripture which is a personal interpretation* (cf. 2 Peter 1:20-21).

Full participation also involves an understanding and appreciation that the Word of God is ultimately the Person of Jesus: *And the Word was made flesh and dwelt among us* (cf. John 1:14, Hebrews 1:1-2). The words of Scripture, then, are the words that God continues to speak to us through His Son, and so St. Jerome could say that "ignorance of the Scriptures is ignorance of Christ" (DV n. 25). No words are more important than those which Jesus spoke and continues to speak over the bread and wine at Mass, but these are only spoken in the context of a faith relationship between God and His People. Isaiah tells us that God's word will achieve its work and goal (55:10-11), but the word must become flesh in our lives to bear fruit, and this demands full human cooperation. God's Word is not a monologue but a dialogue. Otherwise there is no understanding the words of Scripture that *man does not live on bread alone but on every word that comes from the mouth of God* (cf. Deut. 8:3; Matt. 4:4) and that *The kingdom of God is not a matter of eating and drinking, but of the righteousness, peace and joy which the Holy Spirit gives* (cf. Rom.

14:17). And this will only come about as Scripture is more and more read and studied, more and more the principle inspiration of our private and communal prayer and more and more the sole guide for our words and actions in daily life. In brief,

> Just as the life of the Church grows through persistent partici-
> pation in the Eucharistic mystery, so we may hope for a new
> surge of spiritual vitality from intensified veneration for God's
> Word, which "lasts forever" (DV n. 26).

Chapter Two: Discussion Questions

1. Why is the Bible the first chapter of any book on the Mass?

2. What is the central core of Eucharistic belief and practice which the New Testament Institution Narratives provide?

3. Compare and contrast the various Institution Narratives.

4. Discuss how the Institution Narratives must be understood in reference to the rest of the Bible.

5. How did the common meal complement and detract from the celebration of the Eucharist? What are the contemporary possibilities for such a practice?

6. Discuss how and why bread and wine are such excellent vehicles for Jesus' Presence in the Eucharist.

7. Discuss the relationship between the Jewish Passover and the Christian Eucharist.

8. Discuss the origin of the Mass: the Liturgy of the Word and the Liturgy of the Eucharist.

9. What further details would you personally wish to know about the Last Supper?

10. How do you explain the lack of an Institution Narrative in John's Gospel?

CHAPTER THREE

'Historical' Participation in the Mass

> That sound tradition may be retained, and yet, the way be open for legitimate progress, a careful investigation is always to be made into each part of the liturgy which is to be revised. This investigation should be . . . historical (SC n. 23).

III. History and mankind

History is as old as the human family and our desire to keep some kind of permanent record of what is happening around us. The fifth-century B.C. Greek writer Herodotus is known as the Father of History because he introduced some manner of a critical method into the recording of such happenings. St. Augustine, in the fourth and fifth centuries of the Christian era, interpreted history in a distinctly Christian manner which endured until the 18th century: the history of the world is the unfolding of God's will.[1] Yet it wasn't until the 19th century, principally in Germany, that history as a science came into existence. All these individuals and their contributions — in addition to countless others — have brought us to our contemporary understanding of history.

A. History and God

The contemporary world views history as a dynamic, ongoing reality rather than as a collection of dusty facts from the past. This revitalized sense of history especially aided the Second Vatican Council in maintaining full fidelity to the Deposit of Faith while at the same time adapting itself to modern conditions. This contemporary sense of history serves to place in high relief the essentially historical nature of God's Revelation, which includes the Church and the Mass. Just one quick glance at Vatican II's Constitution on Divine Revelation (*Dei Verbum*) shows that already, in the second paragraph, the plan of God's Revelation is being described in predominantly biblical language as a history of salvation,. and further on as that very "tradition which comes from the apostles" and "develops in the Church with the help of the Holy Spirit. . . . For, as the centuries succeed one another, the Church constantly moves forward toward the fullness of divine truth until the words of God reach their complete fulfillment in her" (n. 8). History is, then, the instrument of God's revealing Himself to His People in such a way that the human and changeable elements, whether in the Mass or elsewhere in the Church, while subject to decay and corruption and hence in need of reform, emerge as not merely extraneous or unimportant; rather, they serve as the privileged bearers of God's loving Word and leave behind a discernible mark on the growth of this Tradition.

B. History and the liturgy

It is something of a truism to say that those who do not study history are bound to repeat it. Father Joseph Jungmann, the great authority in the field of the history of the liturgy, applies this and similar insights to the study of the Mass:

> We cannot properly evaluate or properly solve the problems of the present and the future unless and until we study the past. And the more involved and profound these problems, the more thorough must be our search into history. This is particularly true in the field of liturgy, for here history must help us to recognize what we actually possess as an inheritance from the past.[2]

In very concrete terms, Jungmann then goes on to describe the liturgy of the Catholic Church as an "edifice"[3] in which the Church has been living for nearly 2,000 years. In "essentials"[4] it has remained the same, but over the centuries it has become more "complicated"[5] and has been subjected to "constant remodelings and additions,"[6] to such an extent that the "plan of the building"[7] has been "obscured — so much so that we may no longer feel quite at home in it because we no longer understand it."[8]

What is Jungmann's solution? Look up the "building plans, for these will tell us what the architects of old really wanted, and if we grasp their intentions we shall learn to appreciate much that the building contains and even to esteem it more highly."[9] Then, as it becomes necessary to make changes in the edifice and adapt it to the needs of its present occupants, we will be able to do so in such a way that none of the precious heritage of the past will be lost and all adaptations will grow organically from the building's basic shape and style.

C. History of the Mass: 1. Beginnings

Chapter Two, on the Scriptural foundation of the Mass, has shown that

> one thing alone is clear: the infant Church was conducting the celebration of the Mass right from the beginning, and that with surprising sureness, with uniformity of rubrics and with the same literal, realistic interpretation.[10]

But, if the scriptural texts treating the Eucharist seem relatively brief and simple, they gave rise by comparison to a wide variety of types or styles of celebration, i.e. rites — yet another indication that the Mass is a mystery and unable to be fully contained by any one manner of explanation or manner of celebration. Three great liturgical centers grew up in the early Church: Antioch, Alexandria and Rome. From these three came an even greater variety of rites, which by the seventh century had generally acquired their basic form and characteristics. In the Eastern Church this greater measure of variety still exists: to mention only a few, the Byzantine, Maronite, Chaldean and Melchite rites. In the western world Rome early came to enjoy a preeminent place, but the Ambrosian rite in Milan and the Mozarabic rite in Spain still attest to this early diversity. This diversity is noted by Vatican II: the Church holds "all lawfully acknowledged rites to be of equal authority and dignity" (SC n. 4).

In the present celebration of the Eucharist according to the Roman Rite, four Eucharistic Prayers can be used. The second of these originates from the *Apostolic Tradition* of Hippolytus in the third century, when the liturgy was still being celebrated in

Greek, then the language of the people. It remains the oldest relatively complete description of the Mass. Up to this time the bishop, the normal celebrant of the Mass and the leader of the Christian community, was generally free to formulate his own prayers for the Mass around its basic elements: Liturgy of the Word and Liturgy of the Eucharist. The ideal of worship was what it remains today:

> when a full complement of God's holy people, united in prayer and in a common liturgical service (especially the Eucharist), exercise a thorough and active participation at the very altar where the bishop presides in the company of his priests and other assistants (SC n. 41).

2. The Mass in the Roman world

The Mass underwent further modification when the Roman Emperor Constantine gave official recognition to the Church in the fourth century. The number of Christians naturally increased. To accomodate these larger crowds, Constantine made available the Roman basilicas, which gave the church building the standard appearance that it retains even to the present. He also gave the bishops a measure of temporal power, and their insignia manifesting this became part of their ecclesiastical dress. The style of vestments, vessels and gestures came from this period, and they were retained by the Church even after the Roman Empire ceased to exist. The celebration of the Lord's Supper accordingly became less of a relatively brief and simple family ritual and more of a formal, public function. Ironically, the communitarian aspect of the Mass decreased when it could legally be publicly celebrated: the larger congregation and larger building did not permit the post-Constantinian Christians to participate in the liturgy as fully as their ancestors had. Although the Sunday Mass remained the chief celebration of the week, daily Masses began to be celebrated in the basilicas, and after the fifth century it became possible to celebrate a second Mass on Sunday for those who weren't able to attend the Bishop's Mass. In the early Church every Sunday was celebrated as the feast of the Resurrection, but very soon in its history the Church set aside a special date for Easter. The Church's liturgical year also grew to include memorials of the saints, and the feasts of Epiphany and Christmas were added during the fourth century.

3. The reform of Pope Gregory the Great

The names and dates of Pope St. Gregory the Great (590-604) and of his immediate successors bring the Roman Mass to what basically would remain its final form, for the first 600 years of the Church's life mark the formative period of its liturgy, even though the Mass did continue to develop in various ways until the Council of Trent. From Pope Gregory came the Gregorian Sacramentary, a liturgical book which influenced greatly the way Masses would henceforth be celebrated in the West. This was not an official *Missal* in the manner of that of Pius V (Trent 1545-63) or of Paul VI (1969), and a good deal of local adaptation was practiced even by those who used the Gregorian Sacramentary. Pope Gregory attempted to shorten the Mass, which had grown quite elaborate in the days following the Peace of Constantine. There were also liturgical books called the *ordo*, or *ordines* (plural), which were instructions regarding how the liturgical rites should be conducted. Various local churches produced memorable formulations of the Mass prayers, and these came to be collected and passed on from generation to generation. The popes during the fourth, fifth and sixth centuries were especially gifted at such composition. In this way the texts for the Mass came about. Thus, it should be kept in mind that books used at Mass and for other liturgical rites only gradually appeared. Liturgical rites and formulas were in existence before the fourth century, but either they were not committed to writing or they have come down to us only in fragmentary fashion. From the fifth century on, "lectionaries, antiphonaries, *libelli*, then sacramentaries, appear in the West. . ."[11] And in the west the popes, especially Gregory, played a great role in the fixing of these formulas.

How did Gregory the Great celebrate the Mass? The priestly vestments were the same as today, but the Pope did not wear a stole. This was probably worn only by the lower clergy, while the higher clergy wore the pallium. Men and women were strictly separated in the congregation. The importance of the homily had greatly declined. There was no Nicene Creed in the Mass, for it was only inserted during the 11th century. The General Intercessions or Prayers of the Faithful had been greatly reduced in scope, for Pope Gregory the Great was intent upon shortening the Mass, but often enough the people's parts were deleted. There was neither genuflection nor the elevation of the Host and Chalice following the Consecration. The congregation still had a part in praying publicly, responding in word and song, bringing gifts to the altar and in receiving Holy Communion. In general, however, this rather long and elaborate celebration of the papal Mass was dominated by the clergy, which included the Pope with his priests and deacons and with the monks leading the singing.[12]

4. In the lands of Charlemagne

If the popes at Rome exercised a considerable influence on the development of the Mass, this center of influence in liturgical matters was to pass to the north, to the Kingdom of the Franks, during the period commonly called the Dark Ages. After the fall of the Roman Empire in the west in the fifth century, and especially after the time of such popes as Gregory the Great in the early seventh century, the general political, social, cultural and liturgical situation of Rome fell on evil days. Amidst the great chaos caused by the mass migrations of peoples into and within the lands of the Empire, the monks, especially of the Cluniac tradition, were destined to preserve, among many other things, the liturgy of the Church. King Pepin of the Franks in the eighth century took the initiative in starting what would become the great Carolingian Renaissance under his son, Charlemagne. His capital at Aachen became the new Rome, and this was made visible in the old Rome when Pope St. Leo crowned him emperor of the Romans in A.D. 800. Charlemagne completed the work of his father, who had brought the Gregorian Sacramentary north and made it obligatory in place of the Gallican Rite that had developed there. Alcuin, the English monk who was very influential in the Carolingian Renaissance, made some additions to the Gregorian Sacramentary, for it was never meant to cover every eventuality. In general, these northerners greatly modified the Mass they had inherited from Rome, and this form of the Mass was destined to return south when Rome was finally able to emerge from centuries of disorganization and upheaval and was searching for authentic liturgical texts upon which to pattern its own liturgical celebrations, which had greatly fallen off in quality between the end of the ninth and the end of the 10th centuries. Thus,

It would be no exaggeration to say in conclusion that during a
critical period, the Franco-German Church succeeded in saving the Roman liturgy not only for Rome itself but for the entire Christian world of the Middle Ages. By doing this, she was
able to repay her debt of gratitude for the valuable religious
and humanistic values which since the time of Gregory the
Great had, through the Roman liturgy, been heaped upon her.[13]

What were the differences between the Roman and Gallican
rites and their respective spirits? While the Roman tradition had
produced a Mass that was marked by brevity and a sober dignity,
the Franco-German tradition developed long, repetitious prayers,
prodigious in number. They began their prayers with "I" rather
than with the Roman "we." They favored longer and more numerous periods of silence. Many prayers were added prior to the actual
beginning of the Mass, and there were many confessions of un-
worthiness on the part of celebrant and people. More numerous
were the incensations of sacred objects during the Mass, a custom
always more common in the East than in the West. From the north
as well came the use of unleavened bread at Mass, the quiet recitation of the Eucharistic Prayer, kneeling during the reception of
Communion and the multiplication of Signs of the Cross during the
Eucharistic Prayer. All in all, there developed a greater separation between priest and people, and this had a crucial influence on
the shape of the Mass for the next thousand years. The Franks also
witnessed to a strongly anti-Arian spirit in their liturgy, and hence,
as a reaction to the Arian denial of the divinity of Jesus, prayers
addressed directly to Jesus — rather than traditionally to the Father through the Son — came to be added to the Mass. This Carolingian period also provided some of the most striking of Holy Week
traditions: procession of the palms, washing of the feet, veneration
of the cross and the blessing of the new fire, among others. The
Gallican spirit reflected the people of that region, but through the
monk Alcuin in particular, it was also influenced by the Eastern
monastic and liturgical traditions, which heavily emphasized the
element of mystery. Thus, even though we must be "grateful to the
Franco-German Church not only for having salvaged the Roman
liturgy, but also for having enriched it,"[14] it exerted both a positive
and a negative influence upon the Mass.

5. In the hands of missionary monks and Pope Gregory VII

With the coming of Gregory VII to the papal throne in 1073, liturgical initiative would return to Rome. His work is normative until the Council of Trent. He further simplified the rites of celebration and insisted upon having his more uniform liturgy followed by the churches of the west. His efforts were generally well-received, and his reformed *Missal* for the Mass was spread all over Europe by the newly formed Franciscan Order in their work of itinerant preaching. In addition to the great increase of saints on the liturgical calendar, a momentous change took place in the way the Mass was celebrated. This was due to the monasteries: the private Mass became the model celebration. It came about quite naturally during the "Dark Ages," when the monks acted as the chief missionaries of Europe to convert the "barbarian" tribes. Although monks were not usually ordained to the priesthood except to meet the needs of the community of monks, ordination proved a necessity for doing their missionary work. Returning to the monasteries, they continued to exercise their ministry of celebrating Mass. The faithful would gather around the priest and his server to watch the proceedings and would sometimes request of the celebrant that a special intention be remembered, for which they offered the celebrant a donation or stipend.

This practice soon spread to the secular clergy as well. In time, then, instead of the central Mass of the bishop or priest, with his flock gathered around him as a community fully participating in the celebration, many Masses could be taking place simultaneously in the same church and often with no congregation. This manner of celebration remains valid today but varies greatly from the way the Mass was celebrated in the early Church. For not only was the auditory connection between people and celebrant broken when the Eucharistic Prayer began to be recited quietly, but the visual connection was diminished when, from the sixth century onward, altars were no longer freestanding — as they had always been before — but were placed against the rear wall of the church. Such functions as the offertory procession, which had traditionally been exercised as part of the baptismal priesthood of the faithful, gradually declined in importance as the priest began to perform most of the parts of the Mass by himself. Likewise, during this time the faithful were no longer offered to drink of the Precious Blood from the chalice but received only the Host, and even this became rarer than had formerly been the case. Thus, the piety of the people shifted from a participation in the whole Mass to an emphasis upon the appearance of the Host and Chalice after the consecration. The people placed a great faith in the fruits of simply gazing upon the Body and Blood of Christ, which began to be elevated after the consecration during the course of the 13th century.

The Eucharist has always been reserved by the Church apart from the Mass, principally for the sick and the dying, but the reserved Sacrament of the Eucharist gradually began to assume a larger place in popular piety. The appearance of the permanent sanctuary lamp is but one sign of this. Also in the Middle Ages the practice of Benediction of the Blessed Sacrament and of the festival of Corpus Christi grew up. From the end of the 14th century in Germany comes, as well, the earliest evidence of the permanent exposition of the Eucharist. Such vessels as the monstrance or ostensorium made their appearance to accomodate these devotional practices. Prior to the 16th century the Eucharist was kept in an ambry (a niche near the altar for keeping sacred vessels and vestments), but gradually the tabernacle emerged as the normal place to keep the Blessed Sacrament. While the worship of the Eucharist both within and outside of Mass increased during this period, one unfortunate circumstance of this whole period was the decline in the reception of Communion by the faithful, to such an extent that the Fourth Lateran Council in 1215 had to make obligatory the reception of Holy Communion during the Easter season. This is far removed from Jesus' command to *take . . . eat and drink.*

The church architecture of this period further accentuated the separation of people and celebrant by the placing of choir stalls, columns, decorative screens and communion rails between them. Stained glass and the statues of saints often filled the vacuum that had been created in liturgical participation. This devotional trend was also visible in the practice of genuflection, which came to be introduced into the Mass as a sign of adoration at such key points as following the consecration of the bread and wine by the priest, and by the people during all of the most solemn moments of the Eucharistic Prayer. Although genuflection long had a very negative connotation for the Church because of its pagan origin and usage, and although it originally had the meaning of penitence and supplication, it gradually replaced the traditional posture of standing with bowed head, which was the sign of prayerful adoration.

6. The Mass and the Council of Trent

The 16th-century Council of Trent ushered in a new age of uniformity in liturgical matters that previously had been unknown. Today Vatican II reaffirms that the "Regulation of the sacred liturgy depends solely on the authority of the Church, that is, on the Apostolic See and, as laws may determine, on the bishops" (SC n. 22), but it has greatly expanded the roles of individual bishops and of bishops gathered together by nation or territory. Yet, if Trent's was an extraordinary response, the attacks of the Protestant Reformers shook the foundations of the Church in a way until then unknown. With the Protestant emphasis on *Scripture, faith, and grace alone*, not only were Eucharistic devotions attacked but the very sacrificial nature of the Mass was denied. As uniform as Rome became in her response to these denials, both in doctrine and practice, so much more varied were the beliefs and practices of the Reformers. In addition to the many other abuses which Trent addressed, high on the list was the reform of liturgical books and practice. The elimination of particular abuses proved difficult for the assembled Fathers at the Council, and so they left it entirely to the Pope. Consequently, the *Missal* of Pope St. Pius V was promulgated in 1570 and largely remained in force until the eve of Vatican II.

His successor, Pope Sixtus V, established the Congregation of Rites as the source of authoritative interpretation of the official texts for the liturgy. Many of the worst abuses were dealt with. The liturgical calendar, for instance, was revised to emphasize more fully the season of Lent and the other main lines of the liturgy, while the number of saints' feasts days, which had greatly accumulated, was decreased. In general, the Council Fathers took the Mass of Pope Gregory VII's time as their model, for the vast bulk of earlier liturgical sources was unavailable to them for one reason or another. The Fathers at Trent legitimately upheld the liturgical practice and piety of their day — shorn of abuses — as valid and licit. Yet the emphasis upon complete uniformity caused the elimination of much diversity in the Church, for all rites that didn't exceed 200 years of age were suppressed by Trent. This response was symbolized in great part in the Baroque style of art which is characterized by a love of elaborate and ornate detail coupled with a subtle but definite movement toward a central focus. The center of Eucharistic piety in this age is thus no better manifested than in the many spectacular tabernacles of the Baroque style which contained the Blessed Sacrament and which were often unmistakably the core of the entire church structure.

7. The Mass and the post-Tridentine liturgical movement

When Pope Paul VI officially promulgated the present *Missal* in 1969, he praised the great merit of the *Missal* of 1570 and all that it had done for the life of the Church in the intervening 400 years; but at the same time, he noted that a liturgical renewal had also taken place during that same period — especially during the preceding two centuries — and this had gained particular strength in the four decades leading up to Vatican II. These developments necessitated a revision and enrichment of the *Missal* of 1570. This revision is not a break with Trent but a witness to the unbroken tradition of the Church. The *General Instruction* to the *Missal* of 1970 specifies this by reference to the fact that Vatican II has the same aim as did Trent: to restore the rites to the "ancient usage of the holy Fathers" (GI n. 6; SC n. 50). This aim of the 16th century, however, was only fully realizable in the 20th century because of the intervening years of scholarship carried out upon liturgical documents, many of which came to light only after the Council of Trent.

This intent undergirding the reforms of Vatican II was not only liturgical but also biblical, historical, theological and pastoral in nature. Renewal in these areas had also been taking place over the preceding hundred years. Pride of place must be given to the 19th century Benedictines in France, Germany, Austria and Belgium. Beauduin from Belgium, in particular, endowed the liturgical movement with its parochial and pastoral character, thus removing it from its more narrowly monastic and scholarly atmosphere. And it was the universal Church, in the persons of Pope St. Pius X and Pius XII, who enabled all these diverse efforts to be brought together and ultimately bear fruit in the reforms of Vatican II. Pius X promoted the restoration of the Church's musical heritage and encouraged more frequent reception of Holy Communion, especial-

ly for children. His accent on the active participation of the faithful
in the liturgy, as the foremost and indispensable fount of the true
Christian spirit, gave support and a rallying cry to the whole movement. In his encyclical *Mediator Dei,* Pius XII furnished the liturgical movement with its "magna charta," and many of its main
points found their way into Vatican II's Constitution on the Sacred
Liturgy. It is only against the background of these earliest accom-
plishments that the full picture of the contributions of Vatican II
can be understood and appreciated.

D. 'Historical' participation in the Mass

In fact, Chapter Three has sought to show that the reforms of
Vatican II and the way that we celebrate the Mass today can't be
understood and appreciated unless one looks at the whole of the Eucharist's 2,000-year history. As Kierkegaard put it: "We live life
fowards but understand it backwards." Thus, to fully participate in
the Mass from the point of view of its history is to necessarily become something of a historian and keep before one's eyes this vast
panorama — not as a mere chronological listing of customs,
events, people, etc., but as a meaningful whole. This requires both
faith and the use of historical method. It necessitates — as
Jungmann has suggested — that when we celebrate the Mass we
recognize that we are not only inhabiting a church building of brick
and mortar and participating in a Mass in the post-Vatican II era of
the late Twentieth century, but rather that we are part of a much
vaster "edifice" of the Mass that received its essential content and
meaning from Jesus in the context of the Jewish Passover liturgy;
such prayers as the *Kyrie (Lord, Have Mercy)* from the days
when the liturgy was celebrated in Greek; its vessels, ministerial
vestments and basilica-form architecture from the Romans, not to
mention the Latin language; such things as stained glass from the
Middle Ages; much of our Holy Week liturgy from the Franks — on
and on and on it goes — and in fact it necessitates our realizing that
the shape of the edifice will constantly be altered as long as the human race continues.

But also, full participation in the Mass takes us beyond what we
commonly call history, for our Faith tells us that the Mass is part
of the even vaster realm of God's Revelation of Himself to His People and of His plan to unite us even more closely to himself, so that

by partaking in the Eucharist we are released from the endless cycle of year following upon year; we enter, rather, salvation history, where the past — the Incarnate Jesus at the Last Supper and on the cross — is at one with the present — the Mass, which the Church even now is celebrating somewhere on earth — and at one with the future — Jesus sitting in glory at the right hand of the Father (the heavenly liturgy), whence He draws His People to their final home. Thus salvation history unites human and divine history as an ongoing story of the daily encounter of men and women with the Risen Lord, whose privileged moment is the Eucharist. This should make it easier to understand and appreciate that the Mass the Church celebrates today was shaped by God in His dealings with such historically conditioned factors as emperors and fishermen, monks and missionaries, battles and treaties, by languages as diverse as Aramaic and English, and by ways of doing things not only in Rome but in the farthest corners of the world.

Chapter Three: Discussion Questions

1. Discuss how the contemporary notion of history differs from the popular idea of history as a collection of dusty facts.

2. Do further research on the various liturgical rites to be found in the Church: note their similarities and differences, and how they reflect the people by whom they are celebrated.

3. Why are the first six centuries of the Church's history so crucial for the formation of the Mass?

4. How does the Mass celebrated by Pope St. Gregory the Great compare and contrast with our contemporary celebration?

5. In your opinion, did the Franks add to or detract from the celebration of the Mass according to the Roman Rite?

6. Discuss how the Mass came to be gradually deprived of its communal character and became more and more the private activity of the priest.

7. Discuss how the reforms of the Council of Trent and Vatican Coun-

e one tradition and yet address diverse problems of very ical periods.

ally speaking, do you see the seeds of possible liturgical abuse arising in the present celebration of the Mass?

9. Discuss whether the idea and practice of liturgical reform began or did not begin with Vatican II.

CHAPTER FOUR

'Theological' Participation in the Mass

That sound tradition may be retained, and yet the way be
open for legitimate progress, a careful investigation is always
to be made into each part of the liturgy which is to be revised.
This investigation should be theological. . . (SC n. 23).

IV. Mysterium Fidei: Theology and the Eucharist

In 1965 — almost two years after the promulgation of
Sacrosanctum Concilium — Pope Paul VI published an encyclical letter on the Eucharist, *Mysterium Fidei*. In a manner
similar to that of his namesake in 1 Corinthians 11, Pope Paul VI
exercised his apostolic authority, both to express "joy and eager-
ness"[1] (MF n. 8) at the many benefits already derived from
Sacrosanctum Concilium for the liturgy and for the whole life of
the Church, and to warn that the success of the liturgical renewal
and the well-being of the Church could be compromised "through
the sowing of the seeds of false opinions" (MF n. 13) — "certain errors in speculative theology and in practice regarding the Eucharist, errors current at that time of Pope Paul VI and still to be met
nowadays."[2]

Thus, in *Mysterium Fidei* the Church has a document that
complements the Constitution on the Liturgy by presenting the
"basic elements of Eucharistic theology"[3] in outline form, and *A
CATHOLIC BOOK OF THE MASS* has the basic framework for its
Chapter Four: A., "What is theology?" and B., a survey of the
Mass's 2,000 year theological tradition. With this consideration of
the theological dimension of the Eucharist, we come one step

55

to the ideal of full participation in the Mass which the
n presents in Vatican II: a Catholic can only fully celebrate
the Mass — the unity of the Liturgy of the Word and the Liturgy of
the Eucharist — if he is something of a theologian as well as something of a *pastor* (Chapter One), a *biblicist* (Chapter Two), a *historian* (Chapter Three), and a *liturgist* (Chapter Five).

A. What is theology? 1. A science

What is theology and its relationship to the Mass? Briefly, it is
"the correct understanding of the Eucharistic mystery" (MF n.
31). This is not only an intellectual activity but is

> the most effective means to fuller devotion to this sacrament,
> to extol the dignity of all the faithful, and to spur their spirit to-
> ward the attainment of the summit of sanctity, which is noth-
> ing less than the total offering of oneself to the service of the
> divine majesty (MF n. 31).

A correct understanding of the Eucharist is thus essential for worthy participation in the Mass, as St. Paul reminds us, speaking of
God's mercy: *worship him, I beg you, in a way that is worthy
of thinking beings* (Romans 12:1), and it has many dimensions.
Most commonly, it refers to the science of theology, to that scholarly work of "professional" theologians which has as its aim: "to
investigate more profoundly and to understand more fruitfully the
doctrine on the Holy Eucharist" (MF n. 7). This involves communicating this belief in ways that are "suitable" (GS n. 62) to contemporary times and thus making them "clear, more obvious" (MF n.
25). This isn't just a matter of rephrasing conventional teaching in
contemporary terms but of addressing new questions raised by re-
cent studies and the findings of science, history, philosophy and related areas (GS n. 62). It also involves recognizing theology's legitimate autonomy, for

> all of the faithful, clerical and lay, possess a lawful freedom of
> inquiry and thought and the freedom to express their minds
> humbly and courageously about these matters in which they
> enjoy competence (GS n. 62).

Finally, the goal of this theological endeavor is not only to stimu-
late the "mind to a more accurate and penetrating grasp of the

Faith" (GS n. 62) but also to motivate the entire person to live this Faith in a more thorough and mature way (cf. GS n. 62).

2. Eucharistic Theology: Jesus Himself

Theology, however, has an even more basic dimension. For the very term theology in its Greek origins means God (*theos*) - Word (*logos*). This we commonly call the study of God, but more basically the Eucharist itself is theology, since the Eucharist is Jesus Himself, who is *the Word of God* — God's fullest manifestation of Himself, God's Final Word who revealed to us the Trinity:

> In God there is infinite wisdom and infinite love. The Father eternally knows Himself with a perfect Word, an expression of wisdom that fully speaks God's full reality, and this Word is the Son. (cf. Jn. 1:1,14). The Father and the Son love each other with a boundless love, a love that fully expresses all Their reality, a love which is personal and living as are the Father and the Son, and this personal Love proceeding from the Father and the Son is the Holy Spirit.[4]

And it is communion with this Trinity, the Family of Jesus, into which we enter when we participate in the Mass. Thus the words of our human theology are part of the response which we make to the invitation to know and love God issued through Jesus. This invitation is not just any word but the *Word made flesh*. Only in terms of His Person can we be said to practice theology, for only in Him can we speak fully and accurately of and to God. This "speaking the word of God" is a loving dialogue, a mutual knowing between God and us, not just a rattling off of facts or the practice of a theological method — important as these things are in themselves. And it leads naturally to a loving and total union with God. Thus, "even if what he [God] says seems contrary to our reason and intellect; rather let his words prevail" (MF n. 17). This was the challenge of faith presented to those who first heard about the Eucharist from Jesus: some said, *This is intolerable language. How could anyone accept it?* (John 6: 60); and *After this, many of his disciples left him and stopped going with him* (John 6:66). Theology, then is ultimately and basically the Eucharist, knowledge born of and in love, and its necessary response is of the same quality: " 'Well . . . finally . . . it isn't a matter of reason; finally it's a matter of love.' "[5]

3. The "voice of the teaching and praying Church"

If the primary dimension of theology is found in the Word of God and specifically in the Eucharist, closely related to it is the "voice of the teaching and praying Church" (MF n. 46; cf. DV n. 10). Because of the special relationship of the Magisterium with Divine Revelation (cf. Chapter Two), it must be followed as a "guiding star" (MF n. 21). Thus it is the Magisterium which is endowed with the special divine charism which can ultimately distinguish between "revealed truths" and "the manner in which they are formulated" (GS n. 62). It is the task of the theologian to bring the fruit of his research and reflection to the knowledge of the Church and particularly of the Magisterium,[6] and indeed, throughout the history of the Faith, the Church has used theology in the very formulations of basic beliefs. The use of the word *transubstantiation* is a prime example of how the Church adopted a word that expresses fully its belief in what takes place at Mass. Even more basically, the very scriptural accounts of the institution are "colored" by theological differences, "for if revelation has become 'theology' anywhere, it is in the gospel of St. John.'"[7] But all the accounts manifest a similar diversity, and this and other examples of "legitimate variety . . . in theological expressions of doctrine"[8] have always been recognized and cherished by the Church and have been seen as "complementary rather than conflicting" (UR n. 17). The Church exercises this teaching authority in many ways, but none is more fundamental and more closely related to the lives of every Catholic than its care for the liturgy of the Church. In this way, the liturgical books of the Church are her basic theology books on the Eucharist, and indeed on all the mysteries of the Faith, for the very fact that the liturgy celebrates them all. The content of the Faith is expressed in Divine Revelation — in both Sacred Scripture and Sacred Tradition — and liturgy figures prominently in both of these. Thus, many of the solemn beliefs of the Church find their fullest expression in a liturgical text.

4. Theology: "Faith seeking understanding"

Theology as a science in the strict sense generally took shape in the Middle Ages, but in its more basic sense of faith seeking understanding it is as old as mankind. Each of us then can (and should) become a theologian to the extent that we use our mind, enlightened by God's grace, to reflect upon the meaning of our Faith. For even if we can't spend hours reading and researching and reflecting because our job or family take most of our time and energy, as believers we all stand under the same injunction:

> *Simply reverence the Lord, the Christ, in your hearts, and always have your answer ready for people who ask you the reason for the hope that you all have* (1 Peter 3:15).

In sum, then, a correct understanding of the Mass involves not only the science of theology but also its foundations in Divine Revelation, the teaching and praying Church and the everyday life of the faithful.

B. A historical survey of Eucharistic theology

Chapter Three noted that the history of the Mass is a portrait in miniature of the whole history of the Church. Much the same can be said of the relationship of Eucharistic theology to the general theology of the Church. In fact the historical and the theological are but two aspects of one reality, for not only has the course of history witnessed to the development of the form of the Mass from the essential core given by Christ, but also to the development in the way this has been understood. Four main eras mark the progress of this development: the Early Church, the Medieval Church, the Tridentine Church and the Church since Vatican II.

1. Eucharistic theology: the beginnings

During the first six centuries of the Church's life, the classical form of the Mass in the West came to its completion. Despite such momentous changes as the great increase in the number of Christians during the fourth century, the ideal of Eucharistic celebration remained the same, a vision that Vatican II reiterated:

> . . . the Church reveals herself most clearly when a full complement of God's holy people, united in prayer and in a common liturgical service (especially the Eucharist), exercise a thorough and active participation at the very altar where the bishop presides in the company of his priests and other assistants (SC n. 42).

This communal ideal of the celebration of the sacrifice of the Mass, which was instituted in the context of the Passover Meal, was the center of theological reflection on the Eucharist for the great Fathers of the Church such as Ignatius and Augustine. And its foundation was expressed in terms of a notion of sacramentality, emphasized again by Vatican II, that was as equally inclusive of the full reality of God's plan of salvation: Jesus Christ is THE sacrament — THE sign and instrument of God's saving power (cf. LG n. 1; John 14:9-10), as the Church is THE sacrament of Jesus ("the Church . . . is necessary for salvation" (LG n. 14; LG n. 9), and as the Eucharist is THE sacrament of the Church (LG n. 11).

The Fathers didn't practice theology in the way that their medieval successors would. They were content to use, for instance, the philosophical categories of Plato and others in describing how the power of God transformed the elements of bread and wine at Mass. *Transmutation, transfiguration* and *transformation* were among the variety of terms they employed for this purpose. Fond of dwelling upon the significance of the natural symbols which the sacraments used, the Fathers were able to remain concrete in their theology while at the same time drawing their readers into the deeper spiritual realm to which these natural symbols had become special channels by virtue of Christ's redeeming passion, death and resurrection. Variety was also a hallmark of this period. Not only could the liturgy be celebrated according to different rites (with their own languages, customs, etc.), but even the understanding of the manner of the transformation of the bread and wine was marked by diversity.

2. In the medieval period

Rome was neither built nor destroyed in a day. Thus, the 1,000 years following the classical period of the Church's liturgy — conveniently called the Middle Ages — do not suddenly begin on a given day. Medieval Christians continued to believe in the Mass as the divinely established meal, sacrifice and sacrament, holding central place in their community life as God's People. Yet, many factors would greatly modify the way that the Mass would be celebrated and understood during this lengthy and varied period.

In these so-called "dark ages" there were many brilliant lights, and these would exercise a profound influence upon the Roman

Mass. The Northern peoples under Charlemagne and Alcuin would modify its native Roman spirit of sobriety and simplicity with their own more emotional and affective spirit. The great missionary monks, who largely kept Christianity and civilization alive and flourishing in Europe during this period, began the practice of a celebration of the Mass which tended to be more private. And even if this didn't change the Mass's basically social and communal nature, the understanding of the Mass — at least on the popular level — was definitely influenced by this manner of celebration. The way of practicing theology was also greatly changed during this period through the rediscovery of the Greek philosopher Aristotle by the West, to the end of the predominance of Augustine and Plato in western theology.

Although the term "Gothic" was first used as a term of derision for medieval art by Renaissance critics who scorned the medieval lack of conformity to the standards of classical Greece and Rome, this style of art — most graphically visible in the great Gothic cathedrals — became over the course of the Middle Ages "the culmination of Christianity's search for a style perfectly expressive of its faith and aspirations."[9] It is a style that at one and the same time provided soaring spaces, to impress upon the believer the grandeur of God and of the Church which transcends this world, but also a very graphic and concrete depiction of the Faith through the lavish use of such means as stained glass, painting and sculpture.

The spirit of this style also appeared in the medieval fondness for explaining the Mass in terms of allegory: e.g., the deacon and celebrant lifting the chalice and Host during the final doxology of the Canon is in imitation of Joseph of Arimathea and the disciples, who took the body of Jesus down from the cross and carried it to the sepulcher. This was an imaginative way of providing the laity with a vision of what was unfolding before them in silence during the Mass, but it served to detract from the centrality of the Paschal Mystery, which is THE meaning of the Mass, and from the distinction between primary symbolism (bread, wine) and secondary symbolism (candles, etc.) in the Mass.[10]

Most significantly, the medieval spirit manifested itself in the concern to investigate and describe in great detail the nature of the seven Sacraments, and especially of the Eucharist. From at least the 12th century, the theological term *transubstantiation* was judged to fully express the Church's faith in the Eucharist: the change of the entire substance or basic reality of the bread and wine into the Body and Blood of Jesus Christ, while the outward appearances — known as species or accidents — of the bread and wine are unaffected.

The term "transubstantiation" was found to express the faith of the Church in the Eucharist and to do so in a way intelligible to the people of that time. In particular, it set to rest the debate that had arisen between an extremely "physical" and an extremely "spiritual" interpretation of the Eucharist. Already in 1215, at the IV Lateran Council, it appeared in solemn Church teaching, and in *Mysterium Fidei* Pope Paul VI reaffirmed its importance for correctly understanding the Eucharist. In sum, a number of controversies, the development of a new theological method and related circumstances combined to produce what would become a "rather standard treatment of the Eucharist as a theological question: the true presence, the true change which takes place in the consecration, and the manner of Christ's presence in the Eucharist,"[11] and this would continue until the 16th century.

Because the term transubstantiation received a good deal of attention from St. Thomas Aquinas, many have incorrectly attributed its origin to him. Yet this is an understandable mistake since, as fully as any medieval cathedral, St. Thomas sums up in his life and work all that was truly great in the Middle Ages. Against the background of one of the most vibrant periods in European and Church history, his philosophical and theological works portray its spirit at its best: harmonious, balanced, systematic, ordered, all-inclusive. And, not incoincidentally, toward the end of his life he wrote a treatise on the Eucharist into which he poured not only the "best of his acquired knowledge"[12] but as well the fruit of a life of faith lived deeply on all levels of his existence, a fact witnessed by his sainthood and by the Eucharistic hymns traditionally attributed to him.

3. From the Council of Trent

What made the Reformers in the 15th century take such issues with the medieval manner of celebrating and understanding the Mass? The fact that increasingly it more resembled a form of clerical prayer than the public act of worship of all the faithful; that the priest alone seemed worthy to fully participate, while the bulk of the faithful were relegated to the role of spectators; that the altar now faced the wall, as did the celebrant, while screens and communion rails further accentuated the distance between celebrant and laity; that the central Sunday liturgy was replaced by a number of Masses celebrated quietly and at times simultaneously in the same church; that daily Mass was becoming more prominent, as more and more Masses were being requested for a special intention and accompanied by a donation or stipend; that Holy Communion was so seldom received that in 1215 the IV Lateran Council mandated that every Catholic must receive it at least once during the Easter Season; that attention at Mass was focused on the moment of consecration, at which time gazing at the Consecrated Species was seen as the time of special graces, and attention was diverted away from participation in the rest of the Mass which includes Scripture readings, homily, prayers of the faithful. . .; that the Mass was celebrated in a language that the majority of the people didn't understand. This manner of celebrating and understanding was far removed from Jesus' *take . . . eat and drink* and from the early Church's experience of the Mass.

The Reformers based their reforms on the threefold principle of Faith Alone, Grace Alone and Scripture Alone, which they opposed to the supposedly Catholic emphasis upon human works, preparation for salvation and the tradition of the Church. They continued to believe in and celebrate the Eucharist in a variety of ways, while in general denying its basic relationship to the Sacrifice of Jesus on Calvary, as well as belief in the Real Presence or the validity of the hierarchical priesthood.

If diversity was the keynote of Protestant celebration and understanding of the Eucharist, then uniformity was the Catholic response. In general the Council of Trent reaffirmed the validity of the medieval Mass, shorn of the main abuses. In an unprecedented effort, it offered a comprehensive and well-balanced statement on the Eucharist that reaffirmed the Mass as a true sacrifice, which in no way compromises the one, unique sacrifice of Christ on Calvary but which, in accordance with the wish of Jesus, extends its fruits through all ages to both living and dead, differing from the sacrifice of the cross only in the unbloody manner in which it is offered. It also reaffirmed the Real Presence of Jesus in the Eucharist, both within the Mass and outside of it; it encouraged more frequent reception of Holy Communion, although the piety of the time didn't favor this, and it reaffirmed the validity of the reception of Holy Communion under one Species alone — for whether one receives the Host alone or drinks as well from the chalice, the whole and entire Jesus has been received.

4. In the contemporary Church

If the spirit of the first six centuries of the celebration and understanding of the Mass finds a symbol in the private home, where it was first celebrated, and then in the basilica, which, although much larger, was still a center of community life; and if the Medieval spirit finds its symbol in the Gothic cathedrals "regarded as the city of God on earth"[13]; and if the Tridentine spirit finds its symbol in the magnificent tabernacles of the Baroque churches, then the spirit of Vatican II finds something of a symbol in the circular church. There have been circular churches since the beginning of Christianity, and the Vatican II Catholic could comfortably worship in any style of church building, but the circular style does underscore the aim of contemporary renewal to achieve greater Christian unity by a return to the basics of our Faith, an essential part of which is the Catholic belief in and celebration of the Eucharist. This necessarily involves a fresh look at the Mass, the Church's communal celebration of the Eucharist, which is at one and the same time meal, sacrifice and sacrament.

(a) The Mass as meal

What is the Mass? Most fundamentally and obviously, it is a meal. Its basic structure comes from the Last Supper: preparation of the food (Preparation of the Gifts), blessing of the food (Consecration), and the eating and drinking (Holy Communion). Its earliest names underscore this dimension: *The Lord's Supper* (Paul) and *The Breaking of the Bread* (Luke), and this was further enforced by the existence of the *agapé* or friendship meal (1 Corinthians 2), which accompanied the Mass in the early Church.

The Mass is not just another meal; nor is it just another celebration of the Jewish Passover. Yet it isn't possible to correctly understand the Mass without recognizing its relationship to the daily meal and to the central Jewish feast of Passover, and realizing that

> All the meals of men both profane and religious find their ful-
> fillment in this meal [Last Supper], because here we have the
> perfection of human relationship, as well as the initiation of
> man into the divine life.[14]

Thus the contemporary renewal of Eucharistic theology has sought to emphasize that as a meal the Mass is primarily an action and not an object. No one normally comes to a meal in the company of others and sits there looking at the food in silence. Full presence and participation at the meal involve partaking of both the conversation (Word) and the food (Eucharist). Both the meal and the Mass constitute one unified action. On a daily basis, the meal reveals itself not just as a routine act, external to the human person, but as an action revealing the very structure of human existence: each of us lives not solely as an individual, in isolation and self-sufficiency, but in constant giving and receiving of physical, emotional, intellectual and spiritual nourishment; on more festive occasions the meal marks human milestones such as baptisms, weddings and anniversaries. Building upon this natural significance which He Himself created, God in the course of the Old Testament chose meals to be the special vehicles of His Revelation about Himself and His Plan to bring His people to salvation. These took place on special occasions such as Passover and the sealing of the covenant on Mount Sinai, and on a more regular basis at the communion sacrifice (cf. Leviticus 3:1ff). The meal was also a favorite Old Testament symbol for expressing the hope that God would one day bring to fulfillment all the promises He had given His people (cf. Isaiah 25:6;55:1-3).

It is in Jesus that this fulfillment began its definitive realization.

For Jesus, at the Last Supper and at every Mass, is both the meal's host and the meal itself. He replaces the Paschal Lamb with Himself (I Corinthians 5:7-8), and bread and wine become the central signs of this continued presence and action in His Church. He takes the place of the Father at table (cf. John 14:8ff), and by virtue of His complete giving of Self on Calvary out of love for God and us, we, through the ages, are able to take our place at the

Christian Passover Meal, members of God's family, brothers and sisters to Jesus and to one another.

And in response, Jesus challenges us to strive for the intensity of presence and action that marks His own role in the Mass, for the Christian Passover doesn't only release us from physical slavery but from the very bondage of sin; not only are we purified from the residue of pagan Egypt by a desert journey, but we enter into the very death of Jesus; not only do we have hope of an earthly abode in the Church, but we have hope of the heavenly kingdom, where our lowly bodies will be transformed according to the pattern of Christ's own glorified Body.

Thus not only are we able to celebrate the Eucharistic meal, but we are empowered to live it out as a way of life, in imitation of Jesus, whose own life is summed up by the image of the meal and provides us with a full theology of the meal.[15] For Jesus is often seen eating in the Gospels, and He used meals as an opportunity for teaching and reconciling sinners to God; the Mass continues this ministry of Jesus. His frequent participation also shows that Jesus wanted to be fully a part of the life of His people, even of His enemies, and even though He was criticized for this (cf. Matthew 9:11-12;11:19). This is a concrete illustration of the Parable of the Wedding Feast (Matthew 22:1-14) where we learn that God doesn't sit and wait for us to come to Him, but goes out into the highways and byways in search of us. The miraculous episode of the multiplication of the loaves is also instructive about the Eucharist — in that it provides a graphic illustration of God's love, which anticipates our every need, and which alone can fully meet our human needs. Faith alone can supply these needs when human resources fail, and the love that springs from this kind of faith is willing to show the same kind of concern for the needs of others. Not only do we look for our *Daily Bread* in a material prosperity, but we hope for and work toward a spiritual well-being which is a desire to help one another (cf. 1 Corinthians 16; 2 Corinthians 8,9), to share all in common (cf. Acts 2:44-45), to be a servant to all (cf. John 13:1-17) and even to lay down one's life for a friend (cf. John 15:13).

The meal is something that we Catholics have all experienced, whether as an ordinary human experience or as the special rite that Jesus instituted at the Last Supper. The contemporary theological renewal of the Eucharist challenges us to understand this experience as a unity, as the gift of a loving God who constantly outdoes Himself in showing His love at work in our lives.

(b) The Mass as sacrifice

If the Mass is a cultic meal, the heart of the Mass is Jesus' sacrifice on Calvary. We celebrate the Mass because day by day the power of this sacrifice for salvation is being poured out upon God's people and the Mass is its special channel. To participate fully in the Mass, then, is not simply *a matter of eating or drinking, but of justice, peace, and the joy that is given by the Holy Spirit.* (Romans 14:17-18). This is but to follow the example of Jesus in all things: *My food is to do the will of the one who sent me and to complete his work* (John 4:34). This must be fully understood when we hear Jesus' words: *If you do not eat the flesh of the Son of Man and drink his blood, you have no life in you* (John 6:53). This means that the Mass is both meal and sacrifice, and part of the contemporary renewal of Eucharistic theology is to underscore their unity and the unity of the Mass with Jesus' sacrifice on Calvary.

In response to Protestant attacks on the sacrificial nature of the Mass, Trent solemnly reaffirmed this teaching, which is rooted in Scripture and the Tradition of the Church. Scripturally we have already investigated the intimate relationship between the Last Supper and Calvary and the whole life of Jesus which embodied a sacrificial spirit (cf. Mark 10:45; Galatians 7:20). In addition, from the theological point of view, the Letter to the Hebrews reflects upon the nature of Jesus' sacrifice and priesthood and shows how this brings to fulfillment all sacrifices performed in the Old Testament.

And, in the Old Testament itself, the sacrifice of Isaac illustrates in a special way the essence of sacrifice: . . . *What I want is love, not sacrifice; knowledge of God, not holocausts.* (Hosea 6:6); it foreshadows the obedient and loving service of Jesus to God and to all men and women. Also, "for all its dislike of the external sacrifices then offered, the early Church nevertheless regarded the Eucharist as a sacrifice fulfilling the Old Testament prophecy (Malachi 1:11,14) of the perfect sacrifice to come (Didache 14,1,2)."[16] Thus, it wasn't only on the basis of the Medieval Church that the Fathers and theologians of Trent and

their successors sought "to explain the exact sense of the traditional doctrine"[17] about the Mass as sacrifice.

There is hardly any religion that doesn't have the notion and ritual of sacrifice, in which some kind of material offering was presented to the divinity acknowledging his power and lordship over
all and the worshiper's desire to belong ever more closely to his
god. The Old Testament is rich in all kinds of sacrifice. Yet, just as
the Last Supper brought all meals, sacred and profane, to perfection, so too is the sacrifice of Jesus unique and *perfect*
(Hebrews 9:14), offered *once for all* (Hebrews 9:26) and completed in the Resurrection; and it is only in the light of the Spirit
that the full meaning of Jesus' sacrifice is revealed and that we are
able to receive of it (cf. Acts 2:32-33). Jesus is risen and will never
die again (Romans 6:9), but He will always be the Paschal Jesus,
He whom Thomas met (John 20:26ff) and whom the heavenly liturgy in the Book of Revelation celebrates (Rev. 5:6). This is the
Jesus that the Church has never failed to celebrate (SC n. 6) and
whom each Christian must incorporate into his very life (cf. Romans 6,8:18ff).

At every Mass we pray that God will accept the sacrifice being
offered. This refers not to Jesus' offering, which has already been
accepted by God, but to the Church's memorial of this sacrifice.
For the Mass and the Cross are one perfect sacrifice. The Mass
alone — as a human work — could not achieve salvation but does so
in essential dependence upon the Cross. Jesus alone is our Savior,
and the Mass doesn't add anything to His sacrifice. Yet, despite
this basic identity between the Cross and the Mass, there is an element of distinction — at least from our human point of view — that
legitimately can view each Mass as a "new act."[18] Thus, as an act
of the Church, the sacrifice on Calvary receives ritual expression
in the sacramental offering of the memorial of the Cross; and
whereas it generally occurred in silence, it receives at Mass a
greater articulation by the inclusion of the special words and actions of Jesus at the Last Supper and of those added by the Church
through the centuries. This union is best described by St. Paul:
*Husbands should love their wives just as Christ loved the
Church and sacrificed himself for her to make her holy*
(Ephesians 5:25).

This ecclesial dimension of the Mass as a sacrifice has a num-

ber of consequences. The Mass is first a gift of Christ to His
Church, and as such it is essentially both communal and hierarchical. As *Lumen Gentium* states it:

> Though they differ from one another in essence and not only
> in degree, the common priesthood of the faithful and the minis-
> terial or hierarchical priesthood are nonetheless interrelated.
> Each of them in its own special way is a participation in the
> one priesthood of Christ. The ministerial priest, by the sacred
> power he enjoys, molds and rules the priestly people. Acting in
> the person of Christ, he brings about the Eucharistic Sacrifice,
> and offers it to God in the name of all the people. For their
> part, the faithful join in the offering of the Eucharist by virtue
> of their royal priesthood. They likewise exercise that priest-
> hood by receiving the sacraments, by prayer and thanksgiving,
> by the witness of a holy life, and by self-denial and active char-
> ity (LG n. 10).

The Mass well portrays the whole Church as an essentially priestly
community whose life is lived out through a variety of ministries
exercised in the one Spirit of Jesus.

Active participation by all the faithful according to their respective roles is especially fitting for the Mass — this is the main
thrust of Vatican II's renewal of the liturgy. Yet, Paul VI reminds
us that even when this is not completely possible — e.g., when the
priest celebrates "privately" in accordance with the laws and traditions of the Church (MF n. 32) — "such a Mass brings a rich and
abundant treasure of special graces to help the priest himself, the
faithful, the whole Church and the whole world toward salvation —
and this same abundance of graces is not gained through mere reception of Holy Communion" (MF n. 32). This is due to the fact
that the Mass is by its very nature an act of Christ and of the
Church and hence by nature public and social no matter the particular manner of celebration. Pope John Paul II addressed himself to
the same ecclesial dimension of the Mass when he wrote:

> The Church does not thus exist, however, simply because
> persons are united among themselves nor because they experi-
> ence their brotherhood. The Church acquires its continued ex-
> istence when, in this continuity of brotherly fellowship, we cel-
> ebrate the sacrifice of Christ's cross . . . and approach the
> Lord's table as a community so as to be nourished sacra-
> mentally by the fruits of the propitiatory sacrifice.[19]

Both as individuals and as a community, we find our origin in God.

Although it is true that the Mass is a source of graces because of Christ's sacrifice, not because of any human effort, and although it pleased God to make us holy not merely as individuals but by making us into a single people (LG n. 9), God's loving embrace extends to each one of us personally and should elicit from us an equally personal response of love. Thus we are not loved by God as an amorphous mass. Rather, that love is interpersonal in nature, and so just as we are challenged to enter more fully into the Mass as a meal, so too must we enter into it as a sacrificial reality and offer our *living bodies as a holy sacrifice, truly pleasing to God* (Romans 12:1).

This ecclesial, yet personal, nature of the Mass as sacrifice has a number of other consequences as well. In belief and practice, the Church has celebrated Mass for special intentions — for both the living and the dead. This poses no difficulties as long as people realize that they have not purchased exclusive rights to a particular Mass. The practice of giving a stipend or donation for a particular intention to be recalled — a practice to which many object today — can be seen as an extension of the principle of the Incarnation. God does not treat us as a mass of humanity, but as individuals with particular needs and desires which can legitimately find their way into our private prayer and liturgical prayer, as long as we keep in view the basic nature of the Mass. Also, Paul VI noted that the mere multiplication of Masses is no end in itself. "More Masses" does not equal "more graces," and necessity rather than convenience should dictate the proper number. Since we live in space and time, numbers are a fact of life, but the mere multiplication of Masses shouldn't be used as an excuse for losing sight of the proper goal of every Mass: a worthy celebration in keeping with the nature of the Eucharist.

On the road to Emmaus Jesus spoke to His disciples about the meaning of His death and resurrection, but they only came to recognize this and Jesus Himself in the breaking of the bread (cf. Luke 24). It is only in light of the Eucharist celebrated by the risen Jesus that the Cross can be recognized with its full significance. Then it can be seen not just as the sign of the death of Jesus, but also as the power of His new life; not just as the sign that sin no longer has a hold over us, but also as the power for His Risen life to fill that void

in our lives; not just as a sign of the separation between God and
humanity, but also as the power that reorients all of our relationships to God; not just as the sign of cruelty and hatred, but also as
the power of love taken to its fullest limits; not just as a sign of
wood, of the tree of Adam, but also as the power of a body fastened
to it that has become the new ark of the covenant, the new temple;
not just as the sign of an event that took place 1950-some years ago,
but also as the power that transforms the bread and wine at Mass
and the lives of those who partake of this food. In short, the Spirit
of the Risen Jesus has transformed the Last Supper of Jesus and
His Sacrifice on Calvary into a sacramental reality where the followers of Jesus can share in His Paschal Mystery through participation in the liturgy, especially in the Mass.

(c) The Mass as sacrament

The Mass as a sacrament speaks to how God operates in the
Eucharist, to how the Mass is a meal and yet doesn't appear to be
one, to how the Mass is a sacrifice and yet doesn't appear to be
one; to how the sacrament places us in the realm of faith but also
in the realm of very concrete and visible signs; and to how in general all the various dimensions of the Mass constitute a living and
dynamic unity.

Contemporary theology has first done this by presenting sacrament in the context of mystery. This places sacrament in the broad
context that it enjoys in Scripture and in the Fathers of the Church,
and as such it complements the medieval attention to the individual sacraments. In reality we see that sacrament and mystery are
synonyms when we compare the Latin and Greek texts of
Ephesians 3:3, where the English word mystery is *mustárion* in
Greek and *sacramentum* in Latin, and when in the Mass itself we
find the word *mysteries* in Penitential Rite C referring to the Eucharist itself, and *Mystery* after the Consecration in the "Mystery
of Faith" referring to the Paschal Mystery of Jesus, the fullness of
God's plan of salvation. Thus this terminology can help us to speak
at one and the same time of the individual sacrament of the Eucharist and of the whole of God's plan of salvation in relation to which
the Eucharist alone has meaning. Mystery is thus revealed as
Someone and Something beyond our understanding, but with the
positive emphasis that they are open to ever greater exploration —

that God has revealed Himself and His loving plan for us so that we might come to know and love Him and one another more fully, and that He has given us here on earth concrete ways to realize this other-worldly reality, and chief among these are the sacraments (cf. LG n. 2). The focus of mystery and sacrament are on who and what can be known and participated in, and on responding fully to this reality through the means furnished us by God. We should thus not only frequent the sacraments and enter more fully into their celebration, but also realize that any one celebration of the Mass is not just a moment in Church but a definitive realization of the whole of God's Plan of Salvation in which we all have our own individual roles to play.

The heart of the mystery of God's plan of salvation is the Blessed Trinity, and the life and love that They wish to share with all men and women. Each of the Divine Persons plays a special role in this plan. The Gospel of John in particular reveals the relationship of the Trinity to the Eucharist in his account of the Last Supper. The Holy Spirit as Paraclete or Counselor plays a special role in the age of the Church, hence in each of the sacraments, and thus is called the Sanctifier. The Spirit doesn't only work upon us from outside but actually enters into us and brings us the life of God (cf. John 14:17; Romans 8). The Acts of the Apostles — often called the Gospel of the Holy Spirit — complements this by showing the Holy Spirit in action in the life of the early Church (cf. Acts 2; 15:28). The Spirit who raised Jesus from the dead is the One who makes the Church and sacraments what they are and what they do. The Spirit transforms us from individuals into the family of God and keeps us together. Every Mass is a reunion of Jesus and us with the Father through the Holy Spirit.

The realm of mystery and sacrament is the realm not of an impersonal force but of the personal and interpersonal life and love of God, Father, Son and Holy Spirit. The special Presence of Jesus in the bread and wine after the consecration is the climax of the Mass. Paul VI speaks of this as the presence that "surpasses all others" (MF n. 38), a presence that is called "real" because it is presence in the fullest sense: "it is a substantial presence by which Christ, the God-Man, is wholly and entirely present. . ." (MF n. 39). Yet, the pope also complements Vatican II (cf. SC n. 7) and the work of contemporary theologians when he speaks of Christ present in the Church at prayer, performing works of mercy, governing and preaching (MF n. 38). There is thus a flow and gradual buildup of Christ's presence throughout the action of the Mass, which demands of us the same kind of dynamic, ever-growing involvement in the Mass and which should extend itself beyond the walls of the church building. This notion of presence finds a good analogy in the example of a person in love, who enjoys doing everything with the beloved and whose love even draws the person to appreciate more fully everything and everyone around him — making all things more alive but as a reflection of the beloved. Also, any number of people and things can remind us of the people we love and serve to bring them closer to us, but there is no substitute for the actual presence of the person we cherish.

If the realm of sacrament is the realm of presence, it is also the realm of covenant. This term might sound too legalistic, but it serves to describe even the most intimate of interpersonal relationships in the Scripture: the union between man and woman. And this is the language in which the Eucharist is described:

> The renewal in the Eucharist of the covenant between the Lord and man draws the faithful into the compelling love of Christ and sets them afire (SC n. 10).

Covenant reminds us that life isn't lived in isolation but as a network of relationships. The Eucharist is at the heart of this network and radically orients all of our relationships to God. It doesn't erase differences between us but bids us put them at the service of others. The Eucharist isn't a private meeting between God and me, but it draws us to enter fully into the communitarian life of the Trinity and the community with which we are worshiping, as well as into the total life of the Church and of all mankind. Hence a spirituality must accompany our participation in the Eucharist which aims toward unity, service and even martyrdom. Real love is expansive, and in the Mass we have a solemn duty to remember all the needs of all mankind in prayer, for prayer is the power of this love (cf. Mark 9:14-29), and it alone will empower us to live all of our relationships to the full in imitation of Jesus.

In the realm of the sacrament we are "first and foremost"[20] in the world of "symbolic acts or activities as signs."[21] There are in-

deed cautions to be observed when speaking of the symbolism of
the Eucharist, but symbolism is crucial for understanding the
meaning of sacrament (cf. MF 39,40,44). Symbol is part and parcel
of Scripture — Jesus often used an image to express His teaching
and to effect a cure. In this way His own ministry can be called sacramental. Vatican II continued in this vein in the presentation of
the basic beliefs of the Church. Hence it calls the Church a mystery
and goes on to describe it in terms of scriptural images. And this is
only to acknowledge that reality is symbolic: there is a transcen-
dental quality to reality which renders it fundamentally open to a
greater reality. This is what Paul describes in Romans 1:18, and
only our sinfulness blinds our eyes to the presence of the Creator in
His creation, of the Giver in His Gift.

The various meanings of the word *symbol* serve to underscore
the importance of symbolism for the Eucharist and for sacrament
in general. In one sense it means that which draws together.[22] This
is the sense in which the creeds of the early Church are called symbols, or in which the cross is the basic Christian symbol, for it
draws together all the mysteries of the Faith in the Paschal Mystery. In the symbol there is thus a surplus of meaning rather than a
lack of meaning which is commonly charged by the statement *It's
only a symbol*. Also the symbol mediates to us this fullness of reality, for humanity can't partake of it in any other way. Thus, Jesus
is the Mediator of God's fullness of life and love, and He chooses
the simplest of signs in the sacraments to channel His life to us.

Another common meaning of *symbol* refers to the ancient
practice of two partners engaging in an agreement and dividing a
coin between them to mark this.[23] The two parts of the coin were
called symbols. This shows that life is lived simultaneously on
many levels and there is much more to life than is at times apparent. The halves of the coin witness to the existence of the realm
of honesty and trust, and life can't be lived on an everyday level unless such agreements are possible. Neither are the parts of the coin
merely coincidental, for they are the chief signs of the contract and
accordingly very valuable, and must be held against the day of the
completion of the contract. In a similar way, the Eucharist and the
other sacraments are at one and the same time the most concentrated moments of God's presence and action among us and yet
they are only a foretaste of the heavenly liturgy (cf. SC n. 8). Also,

symbols are always ultimately personal. The human body itself is our main symbol, and Jesus Himself used it to reveal His divinity. He further empowered it to be the source of salvation for all — the instrument to know and love God, one another, ourselves and all created things in an unlimited manner.

(d) The Mass as word

No treatment of the theology of the Eucharist is complete without reference to the "word." On the theological level it is essential to remember that even though words are the primary tools of the theologian, they are not merely intellectual in character. Rather, they are so humanly important because they convey the full gamut of human experience — emotions as well as ideas. After the human body itself, the word is the most basic of human symbols. Unfortunately, it has somewhat suffered in the Catholic tradition because the Protestants have popularly been called the Church of the Word and the Catholics the Church of the Sacraments. This is a false dichotomy, because the word is part of every sacrament besides being something of a sacrament itself. Thus, when the priest baptizes he pours water and says *I baptize you* and at Mass he takes hold of the bread and wine and says *This is my body. . . . This is my blood.* These words are part of that "outward sign instituted by Christ to give grace" — the traditional definition of a sacrament.

The importance of the word is well attested by the very existence of Scripture as a whole, as well as by specific parts of it. Isaiah 55 speaks of the special efficacy of the word in the Old Testament, and Hebrews 4 complements this in the New Testament. Genesis 1 witnesses to the creative Word of God, while Exodus 20 (and following) contain the words of the Covenant. There is, as well, the Word of God heralded by the prophets and contained in Israel's wisdom literature, and these Words of God all lead up to and are fulfilled in Jesus, who is THE Word of God. In Him the Word of God is revealed as the knowledge and presence and activity of God, and so we can have absolute trust in His Word because we know that God will do what He says — a perfect reflection of His loving Person. And so it was that Jesus, unlike the scribes, spoke with authority and His words were able to calm the storm, heal the diseased, silence the enemy and convert the sinner. And so it is that

Divine Revelation is defined by the Church as a unity of words and deeds that reveal to us "the deepest truth about God" (DV n. 2), and that the Word of God is so solemnly revered at the liturgy and in the whole life of the Church. Nor is this Word of God only the external written or spoken Word which was set down through the special workings of the Holy Spirit, but also it is the internal Word which God speaks to our hearts — a loving embrace that makes our hearts more receptive to hearing the Word and making it a part of our lives.

Only an in-depth appreciation of the Word will give us the full vision of what constitutes a sacrament and the Sacrament of the Eucharist in particular. This will help us to overcome our blindness to the fact that the whole world is sacramental — that it conveys to us the knowledge and the presence and the activity of God (cf. Romans 1:19ff; Ephesians 1:15ff).

C. 'Theological' participation in the Mass

Often the Bible uses the image of light. The Eucharist, the center of our life in the Church, can thus aptly be compared to the greatest of lights, the sun. For without the sun life on earth would be impossible, and yet we can't look directly at it without damaging our eyes. In a similar way, life in the Church would be unthinkable without the Mass, and yet as a mystery of the Faith it isn't possible to look at it directly with our human eyes. For we are blinded by the mystery unless we look at it through the eyes of faith, a manner that is indirect as far as human sight goes. Thus, there will never be a "complete, rational explanation"[24] of the Mass.

Yet, as St. Paul reminds us, we must worship God *in a way that is worthy of thinking beings* (Romans 12:1), and St. Thomas Aquinas adds that " 'Man cannot give consent in faith to what is proposed to him unless he *to some extent understands it.*' "[25] It is in this spirit that Chapter Four has presented full participation in the Mass as involving a "correct understanding" (MF n. 31) of the Eucharist: that to a certain extent each of us must be a theologian. As human beings it is a necessity because it is of the essence of our human existence that we not only act but reflect upon this action as well. As Christians it is a necessity because we profess the Mass to be at the center of our life in the Church, and by our reflection we can more fully enter into it, and make the celebration all that it should be. Also, by having some knowledge of the 2,000-year theological tradition of the Mass this effort is greatly aided. It is important to remember, moreover, that there is no escape from such an effort, for practice alone constitutes a kind of understanding; e.g., it is more than a little problematical when we profess the Mass to be a celebration of the whole community but only a portion of the community takes an active part in it, or when we profess the Mass to be a meal but few receive Holy Communion. In sum, this theological endeavor, arising out of all Catholics' reflection upon the meaning of the Faith in their lives, will bring us closer to the Eucharistic Mystery which "stands at the heart and center of the liturgy, since it is the font of life by which we are cleansed and strengthened to live not for ourselves but for God, and to be united in love among ourselves" (MF n. 3). And it will help us to see that it is "Only from the Eucharistic dogma, precisely understood and totally lived," that there can come forth "the true meaning of Christian existence, the strength of the religious vocation, the authentic commitment to the transformation of society, the enlightened sense of unity in Christ, in truth and in charity."[26]

Chapter Four: Discussion Questions

1. Discuss the various dimensions of the word *theology*.

2. Why and how are the doctrines of the Church and the theology of the Church distinct and yet closely related?

3. What are the main elements of a balanced theology of the Eucharist, and how does *Mysterium Fidei* aid in providing an outline of this?

4. How has theology so richly contributed to the life of the Church, especially to the liturgy?

5. Compare and contrast in the various historical periods the prevailing understandings of the Eucharist. Were they all well-balanced? Are there any imbalances in current understandings of the Eucharist?

6. What are some of the ways in which the Eastern and Western Churches could learn more fully from each other?

7. Why is the term *transubstantiation* still important for the Catholic understanding of the Eucharist?

8. Discuss the state of the liturgy on the eve of the Protestant Reformation. Did the Reformers reform or deform it?

9. Why and how did the Tridentine reform lead to the flowering of the Counter-Reformation in the Catholic Church, but also to the appearance of many abuses in the liturgy. Can any reform be permanent?

10. Why is the theological renewal of the last century so important to the liturgical reform of Vatican II?

11. How has Vatican II's concern for greater unity among Catholics, Christians and non-Christians been furthered by the reform of the liturgy?

12. How is it possible to extend into the whole of our lives the aspects of meal, sacrifice and sacrament which characterize the Mass?

13. Is the Sunday Mass the center of your parish's life?

14. The Church first celebrated the Mass in private homes. How can we make the Mass more of a familial celebration, considering large congregations, diversity of people, etc.

CHAPTER FIVE

'Liturgical' Participation in the Mass

> That sound tradition may be retained, and yet the way be open for legitimate progress, a careful investigation is always to be made into each part of the liturgy which is to be revised. . . . Also, the general laws governing the structure and meaning of the liturgy must be studied. . . (SC n. 23).

V. The liturgy constitution: something new, something old

To mark the 20th anniversary of the promulgation of *Sacrosanctum Concilium*, Vatican II's Constitution on the Sacred Liturgy, the National Conference of Catholic Bishops, in November 1983, issued a pastoral statement entitled *The Church at Prayer: A Holy Temple of the Lord*. The Bishops remind us that the "liturgical program"[1] provided by Vatican II *"continues to be our program for the Church in the United States of America,* for its growth and vitality, for its participation in the great work of the redemption and reconciliation accomplished in Jesus Christ."[2] And, with a consideration of this Constitution — its contents and spirit — we come a step closer to the ideal of full participation in the Mass which the Church presents in Vatican II: that each Catholic must be something of a *liturgist,* as well as something of a *pastor, biblicist, historian* and *theologian*.

This contemporary liturgical renewal does not cast a cloud over the Missal of Pius V, the fruit of the reform of the Council of Trent, but rather the Missal of 1970 "complements"[3] this earlier achievement. Nor did the Missal of 1970 appear suddenly; rather, the great liturgical progress that has taken place during the past twenty years witnesses to the fact that it was no accident that the liturgy was the "first subject to be examined"[4] by the Council. As the Council said of the occasion. "Zeal for the promotion and restoration of the liturgy is rightly held to be a sign of the providential dispositions of God in our time, as a movement of the Holy Spirit in His Church" (SC n. 43). Humanly speaking, however, and for all practical purposes, SC was substantially written in the 1961-1962 Preparatory Liturgy Commission that preceded the opening of the Council[5] and enjoyed a relatively easy and speedy passage on the Council floor, a sign that the movement for liturgical reform and renewal enjoyed wide support.[6]

A. The constitution and the science of liturgy

The Missals of 1570 and 1970 "both embrace one and the same tradition,"[7] but Vatican II has been able to realize liturgical progress because of "the progress of liturgical science in the last four centuries since the Council of Trent which has certainly prepared the way."[8] In the early Church there was no need for liturgical science, but as early as the fourth century great saints like Ambrose and Cyril of Jerusalem felt it necessary to provide explanations of the liturgy. The passage of time made this even more imperative, since "the spontaneity and communal awareness of the early times gave way to inactivity and disinterestedness."[9] This was due to several factors: 1) the language of the people was no longer the language of liturgy; 2) the liturgy developed a very elaborate ceremonial; 3) only a small portion of the faithful took an active part in the liturgy, and 4) there developed a rather mechanical view of the sacraments which demanded a minimum of participation and encouraged a rather passive devotional presence.

Thus gradually did liturgical science develop to meet the needs of the Church. It enjoyed a particular flowering in the 19th century when its renewal paralleled advances in the areas of Scripture, history and theology. This is the science which SC refers to as "the general laws governing the structure and meaning of the liturgy" (SC n. 23) and which can more fully be described as

> that branch of theology concerned with the scientific study of liturgical rites, texts, symbols and actions that make up the worship of the Church. It studies the liturgies of the past and present in order to help the celebration of the future.[10]

It was the contributions of this liturgical science that gave the liturgical movement its solid foundation and enabled it to flower in the Second Vatican Council.

B. The constitution: its content and spirit

This treatment of *SC* serves further to place the Mass into its wider context as part of the liturgy of the Church. A quick glance at the contents of *SC* reveals the scope of what this entails: After a brief introduction (numbers 1-4), chapter one deals with the general principles for the restoration and promotion of the Sacred Liturgy (n. 5 - n. 46); chapter two with the Most Sacred Mystery of the Eucharist (n. 47 - n. 58); chapter three with the other sacraments and sacramentals (n. 59 - n. 82); chapter four with the Divine Office (n. 83 - n. 101); chapter five with the liturgical year (n. 102 - n. 111); chapter six with sacred music (n. 112 - n. 121), chapter seven with sacred art and sacred furnishings (n. 122 - n. 130), and an appendix with the revision of the liturgical calendar. In addition to speaking of the contents of the Constitution, it is also possible to speak of its spirit, and thus basically of the spirit of the liturgy itself. Several key passages in *SC*'s chapter one refer to this spirit (n. 14, n. 17, n. 29, n. 37) and identify it as a spirit that is *pastoral, "educative"* (SC n. 33) or *scholarly, doctrinal, Christocentric, scriptural, ecclesial, hierarchical* and *spiritual.* All of these characteristics emerge from the contents of *SC* and thus from the very nature of the liturgy. None exists in isolation, but they exist together as a unity. This list does not claim to exhaust the entire meaning of the liturgy, nor is the order of the listings an expression of their relative importance. This listing does provide a convenient framework for discussing the nature of the liturgy, the subject of this Chapter Five of *A CATHOLIC BOOK F THE MASS.*

1. Pastoral in nature

"Pastoral" was a favorite term of Vatican II. In reference to the liturgy and *SC*, it means that the Council called for the various rites of the Church — the Roman and countless others — to be "carefully and thoroughly revised in the light of sound tradition," urging "that they be given new vigor to meet the circumstances and needs of modern times" (SC n. 4). And the reason for this is: "In order that the Christian people may more securely derive an abundance of graces from the sacred liturgy" (SC n. 21). In this work of promotion and restoration of the liturgy, the "aim to be considered before all else" was the "full and active participation by all the people" (SC n. 14). Accordingly, texts and rites were to be "drawn up so that they express more clearly the holy things which they signify" (SC n. 21) and be distinguished by a "noble simplicity" (SC n. 34), a brevity and clarity "unencumbered by useless repetitions" (SC n. 34); that all this be done so that the Christian people could be able as far as possible "to understand them with ease" (SC n. 21) and without much explanation (cf. SC n. 34). And the Council called for the liturgical books to be revised "as soon as possible" (SC n. 25).

Concretely, this resulted in the liturgy having a greater and more varied amount of Scripture within its rites (SC n. 35). The homily is to be seen as "part of the liturgical service" (SC n. 35). The use of Latin is to be preserved in the Latin rites (SC n. 36), but the "use of the mother tongue" is to be encouraged, since it "may frequently be of great advantage to the people" (SC n. 36). In perhaps some of the most revolutionary parts of *SC*, the Council declared that the Church has "no wish to impose a rigid uniformity in matters which do not involve the faith or the good of the whole community" (SC n. 37), and hence revisions of liturgical books are to "allow for legitimate variations and adaptations to different groups, regions and peoples, especially in mission lands" (SC n. 38). It was recognized that at times an "even more radical adaptation of the liturgy" (SC n. 40) was needed, and this could include admitting to the liturgy "elements from the traditions and genius of individual peoples" (SC n. 40). Toward this end, there were to be carried out "necessary preliminary experiments over a determined period of time among certain groups" (SC n. 40). To aid in this and the ongoing work of liturgical renewal, a "liturgical commission" (SC n. 44) was to be set up "to regulate pastoral-liturgical action throughout the territory, and to promote studies and necessary experiments whenever there is a question of adaptation. . ." (SC n. 44). Also, commissions on sacred liturgy (SC n. 45) and on sacred music and art (SC n. 46) should be set up in a diocese or among several dioceses. The liturgy can be televised and broadcast as long as this is carried out in the proper manner (SC n. 20).

The pastoral nature of the liturgy and of *SC* find their origin in

Jesus the Good Shepherd — *Pastor* in Latin (cf. SC n. 2; John 10). This role of pastor which Jesus handed on also entails being a traditionalist (SC n. 4), and this applies to the liturgy as it does to all else in the Church. The pastoral character of Vatican II manifested itself in a special concern to revise and promote the liturgy, but this was part of a broader purpose:

> to intensify the daily growth of Catholics in Christian living; to make more responsive to the requirements of our times those Church observances which are open to adaptation; to nurture whatever can contribute to the unity of all who believe in Christ; and to strengthen those aspects of the Church which can help summon all of mankind into her embrace. Hence the Council has special reasons for judging it a duty to provide for the renewal and fostering of the liturgy (SC n. 1).

Thus in "getting back to basics" in the Church — to the rock bottom of the unity of the Church — it necessarily will foster a spirit of ecumenism to Christian and non-Christian alike, for God wishes all men and women to be saved. Nor did this pastoral renewal of the liturgy and of the Church in general come about completely spontaneously, but it was the fruit of "careful investigation" (SC n. 23) into the nature of the liturgy. The clergy — as the successors in a special way of Jesus the Pastor — have the special obligation to cultivate this pastoral spirit in all of their work for God's People (cf. SC n. 17, 18).

2. Scholarly or educative in nature

The realm of the "pastoral" is often placed in opposition to the dimension of the scholarly, but Vatican II put aside such false conceptions when it laid down that careful, scholarly investigations must precede all pastoral action (cf. SC n. 23). Thus the foundation for the pastoral Second Vatican Council was laid by the liturgical movement that had gained particular strength a century earlier. The scholarly nature of this renewal of the liturgy didn't serve to make the liturgy more complicated but rather to simplify it and make it more comprehensible to the average person (cf. SC n. 21, n. 34). And it especially emphasized rendering the Word of God and the general language of the liturgy more accessible to all the people who participate in the liturgy (cf. SC n. 35, n. 36).

Another dimension of this scholarly nature of *SC* and of the liturgy is what *SC* refers to as the "educative" (SC n. 33) nature of the liturgy. Even though the liturgy was to be simplified so that the connection between words and rites be particularly apparent (SC n. 35), there is still a great need for education in liturgical matters. Such instruction, in a general sense, naturally comes about from Vatican II's reemphasis upon Scripture, the homily and the use of the vernacular languages (cf. SC n. 33, n. 35), but in a particular way it is necessary as a preparation for the implementation of all reforms (SC n. 19).

The clergy bear a special responsibility in this area of the scholarly and educative nature of the liturgy. For not only must they seek "to understand ever more deeply what it is that they do when they perform sacred rites" (SC n. 18), but they must seek to do the same for their flocks (SC n. 19). A solid liturgical training in the seminary will help them to accomplish this (SC n. 14 - 17), and this must be continued for those priests who are at work in "the Lord's vineyard" (SC n. 18). The clergy must learn how to "observe liturgical laws" (SC n. 17), and that "when the liturgy is celebrated, more is required than the mere observance of laws governing valid and licit celebration" (SC n. 11). The clergy must also strive "to live the liturgical life and to share it with the faithful. . ." (SC n. 18, n. 19), and "not only in word but also by example" (SC n. 19). This "liturgical formation" (SC n. 17) must be imparted by professors properly trained for this work (SC n. 15), and the subject of liturgy must be treated in relation to all of its dimensions — theological, historical, spiritual, pastoral and juridical — and in relation to all other areas of the Faith (SC n. 16).

Another dimension of the educative nature of the liturgy is sounded when *SC* lays down that all those who exercise various ministries at the liturgy — e.g., lectors, acolytes, etc. — "must be trained to perform their functions" (SC n. 29). "Experts" (SC n. 40, n. 44) are to be employed in the work of reform according to their area of competence. Commissions on the liturgy, sacred music and sacred art are to be established to enhance the liturgical life of the diocese (SC n. 44, n.46).

3. Doctrinal in nature

The liturgy is not a merely human work. God has given us this great gift in which " 'the work of our redemption is exercised' " (SC n. 2), and He alone can tell us fully what it is. Thus, the Mass is a matter of faith, with a doctrinal dimension, and *SC* succinctly presents this, drawing forth from it those principles and norms which govern the promotion and restoration of the liturgy (SC n. 3). The Mass is central to our Catholic Faith, the "very heartbeat" of the Catholic community and the Church's "entire spiritual wealth" (PO n. 5), and thus in the doctrine concerning the Mass all the mysteries of the Faith come into play (cf. SC n. 16). Thus, to survey the doctrine underlying the liturgy would be to repeat all of *SC* or indeed all of the Faith, since it all leads to the Eucharist and has its center there (cf. SC n. 7, n. 10). From the doctrinal point of view, it is especially important to note that participation by all the people in the liturgy isn't a matter of democratic principle but of Christian principle, and it didn't originate in the 20th century but has been with us since the beginning of the Church. "Such participation by the Christian people as 'a chosen race, a royal priesthood, a holy nation, a purchased people' (1 Peter 2:9; cf. 2:4-5), is their right and duty by reason of their baptism" (SC n. 14). In this and other matters pertaining to the liturgy, Vatican II is careful to note the parts of the Mass which by doctrine are "divinely instituted" and those which are "subject to change" and "ought to be changed with the passing of time. . ." (SC n. 21).

4. Christocentric in nature

The liturgy requires the full participation of all those who are present, but the liturgy is above all else the work of Jesus Christ, an exercise of His priestly office, and because of this "a sacred action surpassing all others. . . . No other action of the Church can match its claim to efficacy, nor equal the degree of it" (SC n. 7). Thus, the earthly liturgy which we celebrate is one in which "by way of foretaste, we share in that heavenly liturgy . . . [where] Christ is sitting at the right hand of God" (SC n. 8). And this is the same Jesus who became man and revealed with complete fullness in His Person the Father, who in His great love wants to free us all from our sins and share His life and love with us for all eternity.

Jesus accomplished this mission of the Father principally by His Paschal Mystery: "Dying, you destroyed our death, rising, you restored our life. Lord Jesus, come in glory." And, just as Jesus was sent by the Father, He too in turn sent forth His apostles to continue His mission in the Church — especially by preaching the Gospel and celebrating the liturgy. And in this not only is Jesus proclaimed as Savior but He is actually bringing about our salvation: at one and the same time we are giving perfect worship to God in Christ and are being sanctified by Him (SC n. 10). This celebration of the Paschal Mystery has always been observed by the Church (SC n. 6), and this entering into the very death and resurrection of Jesus by every Christian means that when a baptism is celebrated in the Church it is Jesus who is baptizing, or when the Gospel is heard it is Jesus who is speaking (cf. SC n. 7; n. 33). Jesus is present and active in the Eucharist in the fullest sense (SC n. 7) but He is also present "in the person of the minister," "in His word" and "when the Church prays and sings" (SC n. 7). It is Jesus alone who prepares us to celebrate the liturgy, who calls us to faith and conversion, both through the external Word of God, spoken and heard, and through the grace within our heart which prompts us to welcome this loving communication from our Creator and Redeemer (SC n. 9). Also, it is only within the full context of the teaching of Jesus that the liturgy is revealed in its full meaning as "one with all the works of charity, piety and the apostolate" (SC n. 9) which made up Jesus' life and should mark ours as well.

Although the liturgy is primarily the work of Jesus the High Priest, it is not a one-sided reality. As Giver of the most precious Gift of the liturgy, Jesus invites a response from each of us. In this sense the liturgy places all men and women in a special relationship with Jesus, traditionally called a covenant. This covenant does place certain obligations upon us (cf. 1 Corinthians 2; Matthew 22), but the full context is not one of a merely legal agreement but rather of a loving encounter with our Savior. Thus the liturgy and especially the Eucharist engage us in the most intimate of conversations with God (SC n. 33) and set us afire with the very love of Christ, that perfect love of the Son and the Father which is the Holy Spirit poured out upon all men and women.

5. Scriptural in nature

"Sacred Scripture is of paramount importance in the celebration of the liturgy" (SC n. 24). For not only in the Mass does it provide us with the Liturgy of the Word but also with the Institution

Narrative, the central moment of the Liturgy of the Eucharist. Scripture as well inspires the other prayers and songs of the Mass, and all the actions and signs of the liturgy "derive their meaning" (SC n. 24) from Scripture. This again reminds us that the liturgy is primarily God's activity, and He alone can communicate it to us through His Holy Word, which is sacramental in character because it actually accomplishes what it says. The liturgy and its language are not a monologue but a dialogue that draws us into God's life, into His Trinitarian Family, where we respond not only with words but with a life of faith. And the importance that Vatican II put upon Scripture for the "restoration, progress and adaptation" (SC n. 24) of the liturgy, it translated into practice through its concrete reforms (cf. SC n. 35, n. 36).

6. Ecclesial in nature

The liturgy is ecclesial in character because it is Christ who is always present in His Church and who has taken the Church to be His dearly beloved bride; associating her "with Himself in the truly great work of giving praise to God and making men holy," the liturgy is thus "an action of Christ the priest and of His Body, the Church" (SC n. 7). Liturgy is then the "full public worship . . . performed by the Mystical Body of Jesus Christ, that is, by the Head and His members" (SC n. 7). The liturgy doesn't exhaust the entire activity of the Church (SC n. 9), but it is the "summit toward which the activity of the Church is directed" (SC n. 10); and "at the same time it is the fountain from which all her power flows" (SC n. 10).

The Church is so intimately connected with Christ and the liturgy that Vatican II spoke of the Church in terms analogous to Christ Himself:

> Just as the assumed nature inseparably united to the divine Word serves Him as a living instrument of salvation, so, in a similar way, does the communal structure of the Church serve Christ's Spirit, who vivifies it by way of building up the body (cf. Eph. 4:16) (LG n. 8).

By her relationship with Jesus, the Church is a "kind of sacrament or sign of intimate union with God, and of the unity of all mankind," and also an "instrument for the achievement of such union and unity" (LG n. 1). This sacramental relationship has its origin in the fact that the Church and the liturgy, like Jesus Christ, are

> both human and divine, visible and yet invisibly endowed,
> eager to act and yet devoted to contemplation, present in this
> world and yet not at home in it. . . and this is so ordered that
> . . . the human is directed and subordinated to the divine, the
> visible likewise to the invisible, action to contemplation, and
> this present world to that city yet to come, which we seek. . .
> (LG n. 2).

So it is that "day by day the liturgy builds up those within the
Church into the Lord's holy temple, into a spiritual dwelling for
God" and this will continue until "Christ's full stature is achieved"
(SC n. 2).

The presence and activity of Christ in the Church find their
focus in the liturgy, which is accordingly composed of "un-
changeable elements divinely instituted" and "elements subject to
change. . . [which] not only may but ought to be changed with the
passing of time" (SC n. 21), when the nature of the liturgy and the
needs of the times together require this. The human part of the liturgy is not negligible because it is subject to change as are all human things, but rather it pertains to the very structure of the liturgy, for Christ Himself had a human body and He and the Church
have chosen the visible signs of the liturgy to signify invisible
divine things (SC n. 33) and to function in a way proper to these
signs (SC n. 7). Thus water naturally cleanses, but in Baptism it
cleanses from sin. Bread and wine naturally nourish, but in the Eucharist they nourish for eternal life. So it is essential that texts and
rites be revised to express more clearly the holy things they signify
(SC n. 21); that all new forms must in some way grow organically
out of already existing forms, and any innovations must only be
made if the good of the Church genuinely and clearly requires them
(SC n. 23).

The liturgy is not a private function, but rather it is the celebration of the Church which is the "sacrament of unity," that is, "a
holy people united and organized under their bishop" (SC n. 26).
Thus the liturgy throughout a diocese is always intimately linked to
the diocesan bishop, and the local pastor represents the bishop in
the parish, which in a certain way represents "the visible Church
as it is established throughout the world" (SC n. 42). So although

the Mass is "public and social" (SC n. 27) by its very nature, and although when the priest at liturgy prays he does so "in the name of the entire holy people as well as of all present" (SC n. 33), the preferred manner of liturgical celebration whenever possible is the "communal celebration involving the presence and active participation of the faithful" (SC n. 27). God chooses to depend upon human efforts to enhance the community actualized so fully in the liturgy, and so SC declares that efforts should be made to encourage a sense of community within the parish, especially at the Sunday Mass (SC n. 42).

As the sacrament of unity, the Church doesn't demand rigid uniformity except in matters involving the "faith or the good of the whole community" (SC n. 37). Thus, the Church holds "all lawfully acknowledged rites to be of equal authority and dignity" (SC n. 4) and seeks to preserve and foster them. Also, the Church "respects and fosters the spiritual adornments and gifts of the various races and peoples" and even admits such elements into the liturgy when they harmonize with the spirit of the liturgy and are not indissolubly bound up with superstition (SC n. 37). Thus in all these ways the liturgy "reveals the Church as a sign raised above the nations . . . [and] under this sign the scattered sons of God are being gathered into one . . . until there is one fold and one shepherd" (SC n. 2).

7. Hierarchical in nature

The Church is a community both fraternal and hierarchical. This is nowhere more visible than in the liturgy, where "each person should perform his role by doing solely and totally what the nature of things and liturgical norms require of him" (SC n. 28). And the liturgy makes distinctions between persons according to their "liturgical function and sacred Orders" (SC n. 32).

Consequently, the "regulation of the sacred liturgy depends solely on the authority of the Church, that is, on the Apostolic See and, as laws may determine, on the bishop" (SC n. 22, n. 25), and "within certain defined limits belongs also to various kinds of competent territorial bodies of bishops legitimately established" (SC n. 22, n. 39, n. 40). And "absolutely no other person, not even a priest, may add, remove, or change anything in the liturgy on his own authority" (SC n. 22).

In a special way the bishop of a diocese is the "high priest of his flock," and it is "from him that the faithful who are under his care derive and maintain their life in Christ. Therefore all should hold in very high esteem the liturgical life of the diocese which centers around the bishop, especially in his cathedral church," and indeed the Church is most fully revealed when the bishop is gathered in the liturgy and especially in the Eucharist with a substantial number of his priests, people and other ministers (SC n. 41).

In the everyday life of the diocese which is lived out on the parish level, it is the "pastor who takes the place of the bishop" (SC n. 42) and he must be especially concerned to maintain this liturgical link to the bishop. The parish priest in effect is responsible for putting the letter and the spirit of *SC* into action in the liturgical life of his parish. He must be "thoroughly penetrated with the spirit and power of the liturgy," and become a master of it (SC n. 14).

All the faithful, by virtue of their baptism, have a part to play in the liturgy, and this participation in the one priesthood of Jesus Christ, most powerfully exercised in the liturgy, is the "primary and indispensable source from which the faithful are to derive the true Christian spirit" (SC n. 14). This participation is both internal and external (SC n. 19) and includes "acclamations, responses, psalmody, antiphons, and songs, as well as . . . actions, gestures, and bodily attitudes . . . [even] a reverent silence" (SC n. 30). The rubrics of the liturgical books must moreover "take the role of the people into account" (SC n. 31). The laity can also exercise their baptismal priesthood by ministering as "servers, lectors, commentators, and members of the choir," for which they must be "penetrated with the spirit of the liturgy" and "be trained to perform their functions in a correct and orderly manner" (SC n. 29). Also, diocesan or interdiocesan commissions on liturgy, sacred art and sacred music — made up of both clerical and lay members — can, under the direction of the bishop, aid the diocese in the regulation and promotion of the liturgy (SC n. 44-46).

8. Spiritual in nature

The liturgy is, finally, spiritual in nature, and *SC* emphasizes this accordingly, because *God is spirit, and those who worship must worship in spirit and truth* (John 4:24). And the Holy Spirit has traditionally been acknowledged as having a special role in the Church's worship, as his title Sanctifier attests. But the liturgy also has a spiritual quality because the Spirit of God has as His ultimate aim to dwell in the hearts of all believers and make them part of God's Family. Thus, every individual's living out of this relationship with God's Spirit in the Church comprises that person's spirituality (cf. SC n. 11). Hence the aim of the liturgical renewal is not only bound up with the external ceremonies — important as they are — but mainly with the hope that the "Christian people may more securely derive an abundance of graces. . ." (SC n. 21).

The liturgy, especially the Eucharist, is at the center of every Christian spirituality, since it is in the liturgy that the Paschal Mystery is most fully celebrated, and indeed through all of our lives we must always carry about in our body the dying of Jesus, so that the life of Jesus too may be made manifest in our bodily frame (cf. 2 Corinthians 4:10-11). Thus, the meaning of the liturgy reaches beyond the walls of the church building, and living a fully Christian life involves a day-by-day and not just a Sunday effort. Living the "liturgical life" (SC n. 18) involves more than just observing the rubrics of the liturgy, but rather it should inspire the faithful to become " 'of one heart in love' " (SC n. 10). And the community experience on Sunday should characterize the everyday life of the parish (cf. SC n. 42). As the 1976 Eucharistic Congress in Philadelphia reminded us with its theme of "The Eucharist and the Human Family," the Eucharist prompts us to recognize that the human family is afflicted by many kinds of hunger, and God's complete love manifested in the Eucharist should motivate us in a like spirit to help meet these needs:

> The Eucharistic encounter with Christ, who gives Himself for others and is intimately present to their hunger, their nakedness and their oppression, demands from a Christian a corresponding attitude to the starving, the impoverished and the brokenhearted. . . . This sacrament is a real sharing in the Spirit-filled being of the risen Lord; what He is by nature, Christians become by grace.[11]

If in no other way, at least a prayerful rememberance in the liturgy for all such needs is called for. In this way all the faithful will move closer to the ideal that we may "grasp by deed what [we] hold by creed" (SC n. 10).

The spiritual life — although always centered in and leading back to the liturgy — isn't confined to participation in the liturgy (SC n. 12). A person must be called to faith and conversion and must then be prepared to celebrate the liturgy properly by listening to God's Word, observing all that Christ commanded and generally living out the faith in works of "charity, piety, and the apostolate" (SC n. 9). Not only must we celebrate the liturgy but we must pray privately to God as an individual or as part of a group (SC n. 12). In a particular way our love for God and the liturgy where we most fully meet Him can be strengthened by popular devotions as long as they are so "drawn up that they harmonize with the liturgical seasons, accord with the sacred liturgy, are in some way derived from it, and lead the people to it" (SC n. 13; cf. MF n. 56-63). Thus full internal and external participation in the liturgy (SC n. 19) doesn't mean that we *earn* the right to participate in the liturgy, for this is beyond our capacities and it is a pure Gift from God. But it does mean that we play an active part in the liturgy, and this participation includes every day and every part of our lives.

Chapter one of *SC* provides a succinct description of the nature of the liturgy, and on this basis it has put forth principles for the liturgy's reform; and Chapters Six and Seven of *A CATHOLIC BOOK OF THE MASS* are in effect a treatment of their application to the Mass. Chapter Two of *SC*, however, advances this work by outlining this application of general liturgical principles to the reform of the Mass.

C. The constitution and 'The Most Sacred Mystery'

Chapter two of *SC* — "The Most Sacred Mystery of the Eucharist" — opens with a concise doctrinal statement of Catholic belief in the Eucharist, centering upon Jesus' celebration of the Last Supper and His death on Calvary, a Mystery that will continue to be memorialized in the Church until Jesus comes again (SC n. 47). Also, the Scriptural character of the Mass is emphasized by *SC*'s general principle that the "treasures of the Bible are to be opened up more lavishly" (SC n. 51) at the Mass and then by the concrete reforms carried out as a consequence, reaffirming especially that the Liturgy of the Word and the Liturgy of the Eucharist are so closely united that they "form but one single act of worship" (SC n. 56).

The pastoral character of the Mass receives heavy emphasis: "so that the sacrifice of the Mass, even in the ritual forms of its celebration, can achieve its pastoral effects to the fullest" (SC n. 49). The fruit of this is that the "rite of the Mass is to be revised in such a way that the intrinsic nature and purpose of its several parts, as also the connection between them, can be more clearly manifested. . ." (SC n. 50). Thus, rites are to be carefully preserved in their substance while at the same time being simplified, being freed from repetitive elements and regaining important elements which had somehow been lost (SC n. 50). Concretely, this is translated into a renewed emphasis upon the homily (SC n. 52) and the use of the vernacular languages, but at the same time preserving the use of Latin (SC n. 54). The Communion rite of the Mass receives special attention with the "endorsement" that the faithful be able to receive the Lord's Body "under elements consecrated at that very sacrifice," with the occasional possibility of receiving the Eucharist "under both kinds" (SC n. 55). These sections of SC also stress the educative character of the Mass whereby the faithful are more fully able to understand the Mass itself and are entitled to receive instruction about the nature of the Mass and about its reforms (cf. SC n. 56).

The ecclesial nature of the Mass is vividly put forth in chapter two of SC, where the chief aim of the renewal — that all the faithful should participate "knowingly, devoutly and actively" (SC n. 48) — is again the main focus. The fullness of this participation is set within the context of the Mass:

> They should be instructed by God's word and be refreshed at the table of the Lord's body; they should give thanks to God; by offering the Immaculate Victim, not only through the hands of the priest, but also with him, they should learn to offer themselves too. Through Christ the Mediator, they should be drawn day by day into ever closer union with God and with each other, so that finally God may be all in all (SC n. 48).

Thus, full participation in the Mass involves both parts of the Mass, the Liturgy of the Word and the Liturgy of the Eucharist, and this was concretely aided by renewal of the homily (SC n. 52), fuller use of Scripture (SC n. 51), restoration of the " 'prayer of the faithful' " (SC n. 53), wider use of the vernacular languages (SC n. 54) and reception of Holy Communion "under elements consecrated at that very sacrifice" which the faithful are attending, at times "under both kinds" (SC n. 55). Also, the clergy are able to participate more fully in the Mass through the renewal of the practice of concelebration "by which the unity of the priesthood is appropriately manifested" (SC n. 57; cf. n. 58). The hierarchical nature of the Mass is also underscored, not only by what has been said above concerning the participation of all the faithful in the Mass according to their particular function in the liturgy and their particular manner of sharing in the one priesthood of Jesus Christ, but also in the presence of regulations which lay down that the bishops must oversee these reforms (cf. SC n. 55) and that they and especially the priests have the special duty of promoting them (SC n. 56).

D. Relation to other sacraments

Chapter three of *SC* does not deal directly with the Eucharist, but it reminds us that the Mass must be seen in relation to the other six sacraments with which it forms a unity, and in a certain sense the Eucharist is "only possible on the basis of the other sacraments, which form its substructure to a certain extent."[12] For along with Baptism and Confirmation, the Eucharist forms the three Sacraments of Initiation. Baptism and Confirmation prepare God's People to take an active part in the Eucharist, the only Sacrament of Initiation that can be repeated, and so to exercise in the fullest way possible their sharing in the Priesthood of Jesus. The Sacraments of Reconciliation and Anointing of the Sick purify and strengthen the faithful that they might more worthily and more fully participate in the Eucharist. Marriage is revealed in all its splendor in the context of the Mass, for the love of God most fully expressed in the Eucharist has been described in both Old Testament and New Testament in terms of the love between man and woman. Holy Orders is the Sacrament which makes possible the very continuation of the Mass.

E. The Liturgy of the Hours

Chapter Four of *SC* serves as a reminder that the liturgy of the Church includes even more than the Mass and the other Sacraments. As well, it includes the Divine Office — now known as the Liturgy of the Hours — which is an essential part of the lives of priests and Religious, and also highly recommended to all God's people. For it is the fullest expression of the Church at prayer outside of the Mass and sacraments, and at times it can even be incorporated within the celebration of the Mass.

F. The Church Year

The Church's Liturgical Year — the subject of chapter five of *SC* also plays a key part in the celebration of the Mass. For not only is the liturgical structure of the Church composed of sacred persons, things and space but also of sacred time. Easter and its surrounding seasons of Lent and Eastertime comprise the central part of the Church Year, which begins with the First Sunday of Advent and concludes with the Feast of Christ the King, while every Sunday is the weekly commemoration of Easter. In celebrating Easter and the Sundays of the Year — comprising the whole cycle of the Mystery of Christ, from His birth to His ascension and His sending the Holy Spirit upon the Church at Pentecost — the Church opens to the faithful

> the riches of her Lord's powers and mercies, so that these are in some way made present at all times, and the faithful are enabled to lay hold of them and become filled with saving grace (SC n. 102).

The Church Year also gives special place to the memory and intercession of the Blessed Virgin Mary (SC n. 103) as well as to that of the martyrs and other saints (SC n. 104).

The revision of the Church Year is to mirror the priority noted above: primary attention must be paid to the feasts of the Lord in which the mysteries of salvation are celebrated during the course of the year. This Temporal Cycle is given preference over the Sanctoral Cycle, containing the feasts of the saints (SC n. 108). Many of the latter feasts are left to be celebrated "by a particular Church or nation or religious community; only those should be extended to the universal Church which commemorate saints who are truly of universal significance" (SC n. 111). Again, the Second Vatican Council did not demote the Blessed Virgin or the saints — their importance for the Faith and the faithful remains — but proper perspective was restored to an area of the Church — the Church calendar — which all too easily falls victim to the abuses that Vatican II set out to correct.

G. Sacred music and art

The topics of Chapters Six and Seven of *SC* are Sacred Music and Sacred Art, and they as well are closely united to the celebration of the Mass. The Church is the possessor of a great musical tradition. This isn't mere ornamentation but forms a "necessary and integral part" of the liturgy (SC n. 112) and gives the liturgy a more noble form (SC n. 113). However, music must always be used so that it contributes to the active participation of all the faithful at the liturgy (SC n. 114). The Church gives pride of place to Gregorian Chant, but other kinds of music can be employed if they are in accord with the spirit of the liturgy (SC n. 116). This applies to the musical traditions of all peoples who make up the Church (SC n. 118). Among musical instruments, the pipe organ holds a distinguished place in the Church's liturgy, but other instruments may also be used if they are deemed suitable by competent authority (SC n. 120). New musical compositions are also to be encouraged (SC n. 121).

The same basic principles also apply to the question of sacred art and sacred furnishings in the Church. *SC* reminds us that the Church has always been a patron of the arts and has always sought out artistic talent to enhance the beauty and solemnity of the liturgy. Yet the Church continues to reserve to herself the prerogative of passing judgment upon the arts, deciding which are suitable for sacred liturgical usage (SC n. 122). The Church desires "noble beauty" rather than "mere extravagance" (SC n. 124). The Church is open to accepting all forms of art, both in the construction and decoration of its buildings, but refuses any art that is offensive to Christian piety, faith and morals or is merely mediocre or pretentious in character (SC n. 124). The practice of placing sacred images in churches is to be maintained, but "their number should be moderate and their relative location should reflect their right order" (SC n. 125). In each diocese the local bishop should give a hearing to the diocesan liturgical commission and to other experts on such matters in the regulation and promotion of sacred art and sacred music. Greater attention is given to these subjects by the *Roman Missal* in chapter five of its *General Instruction*: "Ar-

rangement and Decoration of Churches for the Eucharistic Celebration.''

H. 'Liturgical' participation in the Mass

Chapter Five of A CATHOLIC BOOK OF THE MASS has presented yet another dimension of what full participation in the Mass
involves: that every Catholic must be something of a liturgist. This
means that each one of us must have an appreciation for the fact
that the Mass stands at the center of the Church, but that it doesn't
stand there in isolation; rather, it is the main part of the Church's
entire liturgical life. Thus, the revision of the Mass took place not
only in response to the pastoral needs of the 20th century but also in
relation to the enduring nature of the liturgy, which has a definite
content and spirit. This has its origin in Jesus, and as God's gift to
the Church, it involves the entire participation of all the Church's
members, both in its actual celebration and in the hierarchy's special role of preserving its purity and integrity. Only in this way,
then, can the Christian live in the two worlds of earth and heaven to
which our Christian vocation commits us and

> perceive that we are not *either* sinners or the body of Christ,
> but that we are *both, simultaneously*. Sinful aliens estranged
> from God and one another, we Christian worshipers are also —
> and just as truly — a holy nation, a royal priesthood, a people
> set apart. Only through the . . . power of the liturgy can these
> two irreconcilable realities be brought together into a coherent
> whole. That is why worship is always an "epiphany" of the
> Church at its worst and at its best. And that is also why the lit-
> urgy moves back and forth between protestations of sin and un-
> worthiness . . . and bold, confident assertions of intimacy with
> God. . . .[13]

Thus, the liturgy is for us a mirror into which we look to see our full
selves, and a bridge by which we can arrive at that fullness. So
even now, though we continue in our sinfulness and our estrange-
ment from God, one another, ourselves and all creation, still in the
liturgy we can dimly see and slowly arrive at that realm where we
will experience the fullness of God's grace and enjoy the intimacy
of the divine and human families.

Chapter Five: Discussion Questions

1. How does your parish liturgy reflect the spirit of the liturgy that is outlined in *SC*?

2. How can we speak of a continuing liturgical movement?

3. How does the Catholic liturgy touch more than the lives of Catholics?

4. How can you make the Paschal Mystery more a part of your life in the liturgy and outside of it?

5. Does the mention of the various modes of Jesus' Presence in the Mass, and particularly the fact of the removal in many cases of the tabernacle away from the main altar, cause you any difficulties?

6. Why and how do human elements enhance the liturgy?

7. How would you describe your parish liturgy — do people participate or do they sit back and watch? Discuss how this can be improved.

8. Describe the elements that make up an external and internal participation at the Mass.

9. What is your liturgical spirituality?

10. How can a parish incorporate concern for social problems into the Mass, e.g., hunger, peace, etc.?

11. Why is it an indefensible position that the liturgy should never be changed?

12. Discuss the importance of ongoing liturgical education for both laity and clergy.

13. Discuss the part that Canon Law plays in the liturgy.

14. What kind of liturgical adaptation has taken place in the American Church, your diocese, your parish?

15. What is the value of a commission? Isn't it much more efficient to have the bishop or priest decide liturgical matters?

16. What part do music and art play in the Masses in which you are a participant?

17. Why are understanding and intelligibility so important an aim of *SC*? Wasn't it better when the whole liturgy was in Latin, a sacred language, and the liturgy was preserved from becoming banalized and too familiar?

18. What kind of possibilities do you see for making the *Liturgy of the Hours* a part of your liturgical and private prayer life?

19. What was the point of removing so many of the popular saints from the liturgical year? Did it impoverish or enrich the celebration of the Mass?

20. A good celebration of the Mass and of all liturgy demands more than the meeting of the conditions for validity. Discuss the ramifications of this statement.

21. What is the place of private prayer in the Mass?

22. List and define all the elements that compose the ritual of the liturgy; e.g., Sacramentary, Lectionary, rubrics. . . .

CHAPTER SIX

Full Participation
in the Liturgy of the Word

That sound tradition may be retained, and yet, the way be open for legitimate progress, a careful investigation is always to be made into each part of the liturgy which is to be revised (SC n. 23).

VI. The Liturgy of the Word and Vatican II

In the chapel of the North American College, the American Catholic Church's seminary in Rome, the art work in the sanctuary gives prominence to the seven sacraments, but along with them there is a panel depicting the proclamation of the Word of God. Today, after the renewal of the Second Vatican Council has given a greater emphasis to Scripture and preaching in the Mass, this is not so surprising. In those years, however, it was still something of a truism that the Protestants tended to give precedence to the Word and Catholics to give precedence to the Sacrament.

Based on the intense scriptural scholarship — both inside and outside the Catholic Church — which has gone on during the last several centuries, and especially given encouragement within the Church by Pope Pius XII's encyclical on the Bible, *Divino Afflante Spiritu*, in 1943, Vatican II confidently acknowledged and then implemented that the "Sacred Scripture is of paramount importance in the celebration of the liturgy" (*Sacrosanctum Concilium* n. 24). This is based on the firm belief that "in the liturgy . . . Christ is still proclaiming His Gospel" (SC n. 33), and that "in the sacred books, the Father who is in heaven meets His children with great love and speaks with them" (*Dei Verbum* n. 21). The words of Scripture have been written down under the inspiration of the Holy Spirit and are thus carefully preserved by the Church, but this same Spirit writes these same words in the hearts of believers who welcome His presence in their lives.

Concretely, this reemphasis of the Church's basic belief in the Word of God has returned to the Mass a more varied and suitable selection of biblical readings, a homily that is seen as part of the liturgy and whose content should come from the scriptural readings and liturgical sources, and both readings and homily given in the manner of a proclamation of God's wonderful works in the history of salvation. This revision of the structure of the Mass has restored a greater balance and harmony between the two principal parts: the liturgy of the Word and the liturgy of the Eucharist, for the Church has always venerated the divine Scriptures just as she venerates the Body of the Lord "since from the table of both the word of God and of the Body of Christ she [the Church] unceasingly receives and offers to the faithful the bread of life, especially in the liturgy" (*Dei Verbum* n. 21).

Viewed from this perspective the words of the Scripture are not only the central focus of the liturgy of the Word, the first principal part of the Mass, but they are also the basis for the liturgy of the Eucharist, since it is from the Bible that the very central words of the Eucharistic Prayer are derived: the Institution Narrative or words of Consecration over the bread and wine. This should lay to rest any false dichotomy between word and sacrament in the Catholic tradition, since the two of them in faith and practice have always been intimately bound together. Vatican II merely enabled the Mass to manifest this ever more clearly by restoring certain parts of the Mass that had either been deleted or allowed to become less clear in meaning and function.

This chapter will survey the various elements of the liturgy of the Word from the perspective of its revised form: that the rite of the Mass be so revised that the intrinsic nature and purpose of its various parts, as also the connection between them (SC n. 50), be more clearly manifested. The ultimate aim of this is that the devout and active participation of the faithful can be more easily accomplished (SC n. 48). Both the whole and the parts of the Mass must always be kept in view: for as is known through historical investigation, the Mass developed part by part from the basic scriptural core to its present state of one unified act of worship (SC n. 56). To the whole of the Mass there is a natural flow and rhythm that depend upon the specific meaning of each part. This naturally reaches a high point in the Institution Narrative, which then most fully should lead to the Communion rite and the sharing of the Lord's Body and Blood by all present. The spiritual life of the faithful — our growth in friendship with God — is the reason for the Mass, both as an act of worship of God and of the sanctification of men and women. God's grace alone has the power to save us, but God works only in accordance with the free response of the individual.

Because the Mass exists ultimately for the salvation of God's People, the pastoral dimension of the celebration of the Mass is essential. This should provide a celebration in which the people can most fully participate and thus attain what is the purpose of the Mass. The pastoral, however, is at one with the faith of the Church in the Mass and should flow from it with the help of scriptural, historical, theological and liturgical study. It is neither something extraneous to the sacraments nor in opposition to their valid and licit celebration. Rather, the pastoral concern of the celebrant is to make the sign-value of the sacraments as visible and manifest as is humanly possible using all legitimate human and divine resources.

A. The Liturgy of the Word: Introduction

The basic structure of the Mass's liturgy of the Word, its first principal part, has its origin in the Jewish synagogue prayer and scripture service. In Luke 4, Jesus is shown taking part in such a service. In the early Church this was celebrated separately from the liturgy of the Eucharist because it was only after a time that the Christians were expelled from the synagogue and had to hold their own similar service, but very soon the two became part of the unity we call the Mass.

In the ancient Mass, as celebrated at Rome, the liturgy of the Word — i.e. the beginning of the Mass — began quite abruptly. In Chapter Seven of *ACBM* it will be seen that the Mass ends equally as abruptly. This certainly is in keeping with the nature of the Passover meal, the context in which Jesus ate the Last Supper, with its emphasis upon haste. Christians likewise eat the meal in haste — in anticipation of the return of Christ in glory. Because of this, any introductory or entry rites preceding the readings are variable and subject to change, for the only absolutes necessary for commencing the Mass are the assembly of the congregation and the entrance of the celebrant. Yet it was a natural development that such rites should develop in the Mass, and that even preceding these there should appear some kind of preparation for the faithful and the priest.[1]

According to the Missal of Pope Pius V, the celebrant was obligated to pray certain prayers while vesting and when he arrived at the foot of the altar. Although these prayers were the products of a long development, they should remain private, and the revision of 1970 has indeed done this. Historically these prayers had entered the Mass through Carolingian influence and had become a part of the Mass when the private Mass had come to be the model of celebration. Yet they serve to remind celebrant and congregation alike that each has the obligation to make a private spiritual preparation. Both celebrant and faithful do this, not only for themselves but for the rest of the community of which they are a part. In a practical vein, this is a reminder that the time immediately preceding Mass is also an opportunity for preparatory prayer.

1. *The Introductory or Preparatory rites of the Mass* include: *The entrance of the celebrant; the entrance song; the Sign of the Cross; the greeting; Penitential Rite; Lord, Have Mercy (Kyrie); Gloria,* and *Opening Prayer (or Collect).* The purpose of these rites is to help transform the congregation from a crowd of people into a worshiping community of the faithful. During the entrance procession — the first of the three great processions of the Mass, which also include that of the offertory and the communion — a song is sung or the entrance antiphon recited. This involves both priest and people, and possibly a choir. The entrance antiphon is the oldest part of the introductory rites, but it had shrunk in pre-Vatican II days to only a truncated remnant of its original form. Ideally, the theme of the liturgy should be introduced by this entrance song. This is already an indication that the revised Missal necessitates advance planning, including the music, if the Mass is to be properly celebrated. This will aid the people in more fully entering into the celebration of the Mass, for merely on the human level, the beginning of anything is a most crucial time. It is a traditional custom, and one in keeping with the spirit of Vatican II's reform, to carry the lectionary in this entrance procession and then place it solemnly on the altar before the start of the Mass.

(a) According to ancient tradition, *the celebrant reverences the altar* with a kiss. The primary significance of this action lies in the altar as a symbol of Christ — as St. Ambrose tells us. For, the altar is the center of the whole Eucharistic action. The altar may also be incensed.

(b) Following the *Sign of the Cross*, there comes the *greeting* — of which there are several options — not merely expressing a desire that the Lord be present but actually a statement of belief that He is already present there. For it is God alone who gathers the people together and gives efficacy and power to their act of worship and sanctification. This reminds the Christian that the Mass isn't just any kind of meeting, but a sacred assembly in which God and man communicate in a very deep and efficacious manner. This is the beginning of the process whereby the people become a community, a sign of the mystery of the Church and of God's presence in them as a communion of faith and love. All in the introduction should make them aware that the liturgy is the "outstanding means by which the faithful can express in their lives, and manifest to others, the mystery of Christ and the real nature of the true Church"(SC n. 2).

(c) *The penitential rite* expresses the belief of Christians that purification is necessary before taking part in the Eucharist. Historically, the first real penitential rite to enter the Mass was the Lamb of God[2] and it was meant, in the eighth century, to accompany the rather long rite of breaking the Eucharistic loaves of bread. Before the present insertion of the penitential rite, only the priest in the prayers at the foot of the altar observed such a rite. Now it is more appropriately a communal manifestation of the need of the whole Church for constant penance and renewal. Again there are options for this rite, and the third form has the advantage of being especially scriptural in orientation. Historically as well, this option is extremely rich, for it joins the *Lord, Have Mercy* or *Kyrie*, a remnant of the time when the Mass was celebrated in Greek, to a litany which bears a close resemblance to its much fuller form in the ancient liturgy, when it occurred after the readings and more resembled the current general intercessions or prayer of the faithful, which itself has been restored to the Mass by Vatican II. In the present structure of the Mass, however, this form of the penitential rite is a chant whereby the faithful cry out to the Lord and beg his mercy in a litany of repentance, and it shouldn't be used to duplicate the prayer of the faithful.

The celebrant is able to introduce in his own words the penitential rite (as well as the "Pray, brethren" after the offertory, the Our Father, the greeting of Peace and the invitation to Communion). This represents a centuries-old break with the tradition of the celebrant not speaking "on his own" in the Mass except for the homily. The Mass is the priestly prayer of Jesus Christ, and the priest is not to unduly impose his personality upon the Mass. Yet this is the opportunity for the priest to pray spontaneously and set the liturgy in the actual circumstances in which it is taking place — not only regarding the scriptural, liturgical themes of the day but also including events in the community and world. The priest's own religious experience and his witnessing to it are part of his sign value as he acts in the Person of Christ.[3] The faithful in many ways take their cue for the spirit of the liturgy from the celebrant, and it falls upon him to create sacred space and time. This he does by separating the people sufficiently from their concerns so that they can enter fully into the Mass, but also by inviting them to add their cares and concerns to the Prayer of the Mass. It is done by the priest exercising his creativity and not merely relying upon the same set formulas. This could be called exercising liturgical presence on the part of the celebrant. For indeed he must instill the proper liturgical spirit in the congregation and set the tone of the celebration by taking care to attain a balance of order, dignity and preparation. Needless to say, this does not include verbosity, ignoring the Scripture and liturgical themes of the day or improperly changing the prescribed prayers of the Mass.

(d) The *Gloria* is part of a series of very ancient hymns dating back to the early Church. For many centuries only the bishop recited or sang it. Only in the 11th century did the priest use it as freely as the bishop. It was also restricted originally to the Christmas season, because of its opening lines which come from the Gospel of Luke. Today it is a part of the Mass in the ordinary sense, used on Sundays outside of Advent and Lent, on feast days and other solemn occasions. The Trinitarian structure of the Gloria is very pronounced, and it reminds us that our worship is part of the heavenly liturgy — such as the biblical *Book of Revelation* exalts — and that our present sacramental worship will eventually lead us to see God face-to-face.

(e) The *opening prayer or Collect* serves as a conclusion to the introductory rites and the entrance procession, just as the prayer over the gifts (the Secret) concludes the offertory procession and the postcommunion prayer brings the communion procession to a close. The priest raises his arms in the ancient manner of prayer, and the people stand as a token of their special attention at this key moment in the liturgy. The priest pauses briefly after he says *Let us pray*, and this gives all in attendance the opportunity to recall their own private intentions, before the priest sums them up or "collects" them in the context of the opening prayer, which emphasizes the liturgical theme of the day's Mass. In this way, silence is seen to have a positive part to play in the liturgy as a time for personal prayer, a response by all to what they have heard or spoken in light of their own concrete circumstances.[4]

Although prayer may legitimately be addressed to God the Father or God the Son or God the Holy Spirit individually, traditionally the prayers in the Mass, like the whole of the Mass, are addressed to the Father through the Son in the Holy Spirit. Because Arius (a Christian of the fourth century) denied the divinity of Christ, prayers in the Mass came to be addressed directly to Christ.

The first centuries of the Mass were marked by a great deal of variety and improvisation. There were essential elements around which this was carried on, but several centuries passed before set formulas came to be written down and handed on. These opening prayers always were to be suited to the concrete liturgical and faith themes of the day and season. Especially from the fourth to the sixth centuries, the Popes composed a number of very beautiful prayers of this type, and these came to be preserved in the Church. It is historically interesting to note that unlike the Prefaces, which are primarily scriptural in origin, the Roman Collects are closer in style and content to the ancient cultural and literary tradition of Rome.[5] Very often only their conclusion gave them a specifically Christian flavor. The Christians, despite their fierce opposition to all pagan worship, felt free to borrow from the Roman world in which they found themselves living. In this way the Church came to use the Latin language for centuries, to copy Roman dress, which at Mass the priest still wears, to use Roman gestures and vessels for eating and drinking, and the Roman basilica form for its churches. Many a fine ancient Roman building continues to exist because it became a Christian church.

All in all, the above makes for a rather full introductory rite, considering that the principal part of the liturgy of the Word is yet to come. However, it can greatly enhance what is to follow if properly unified with it.

2. The private or communal reading of the *Word of God* is an end in itself because it is the spiritual nourishment of Christians. But in the context of the Liturgy this is even more pronounced. In the Mass the Word of God is addressed to all and to each individually, as a personal message of God's love to draw closer to Him and one another. This is repeated throughout all of the Bible. The Scriptures are no mere record of past events, but they are Christ Himself, sent by the Father in the Spirit, extending again and again in every age this same invitation to believe in and hope in and love God. The faithful have been gathered by the Word of God, and now in a special way they listen to Him and about Him: to all He will continue to do for men and women who open their hearts to His entrance. This memorial of God's Word helps to solidify the faithful more and more into a community, realizing again their common origin and goal. It aids the deeper personal involvement that is to follow in the liturgy of the Eucharist. Having the Scriptures read in the vernacular was designed to facilitate this emphasis upon the Word of God as a communication between God and man rather than a monologue on God's part. Vatican II has made the whole Liturgy of the Word more coherent and intelligible, restoring to it an integrity to which it is entitled, for although its natural conclusion is to lead into the liturgy of the Eucharist, it is not primarily a preparation for it.[6]

(a) *Three readings* is the usual complement, but this has varied from rite to rite. In the early Church the "Gospels and the Epistles were a continuous reading."[7] In the revised lectionary there is a three-year cycle for Sundays and holy days and a two-year cycle for the weekdays. In this way practically all four gospels can be read in their entirety over the whole of the three-year cycle or in any one of the two-year weekly cycles. The first reading is traditionally from the Old Testament, except during the Easter season when it comes from the Acts of the Apostles. The second reading comes from the New Testament, often emphasizing some moral instruction relevant to the Christian life. Between the first two readings there is a psalm and response (gradual) which also has its origin in the Jewish synagogue liturgy. In the beginning the Church sang or recited the psalm in its entirety, and on occasion it sufficed as one of the readings. Customarily the Gospel and the first reading are linked by theme, and before the proclamation of the Gospel the verse and Alleluia are sung, except during the season of Lent. The Alleluia, of Jewish origin, conveys the glory of the coming Lord, who is to become present in a special way in the Mass when the Gospel is proclaimed.

The actual reading of the Scriptures is done by ministers, except for the Gospel, which since the fourth century has been reserved to the deacon or priest. The reverence with which this is to be done can be highlighted by carrying the Gospel book in procession from the altar to the stand where it is to be proclaimed. It is essential that the Gospel be proclaimed and not merely read. For proclamation conveys that this moment of the liturgy is an event of salvation. God is intervening here, as He has done in all salvation history, and is calling His people to a special response of faith and hope and love. In the Bible, word and event are inextricably mixed — the word makes clear what the event is bringing about. All the readings should of course be read well — loudly and clearly and with a sense that it is God who is actually communicating with His people. One should as reverently handle the Word of God as one would touch the consecrated Bread and Wine or the other sacred objects of the sacraments. This realization can be heightened by the lectors and celebrant reminding themselves that the Word of God covers a vast spectrum of experience — history, poetry, prophecy, wisdom literature, among others — and these should be read accordingly. This experience isn't just any kind of experience but was inspired by God and is thus a grace-filled communication. Through people and events, God speaks not only about Himself but communicates His very Self. As a testimony of the communal life of the Christian community, it should be so read — that it might inspire others in the Church to do the same. Likewise, although it does give a measure of information about God, its nourishment is more in the manner of food. For, as Jesus quoted the Old Testament to the devil, Man does not live on bread alone but on every word that comes from the mouth of God (cf. Deuteronomy 8:3). Accordingly, the Word of God should be handled as carefully and well as food that is being prepared for honored guests. Times for silence between the readings and responses should be provided. This allows for a blending of private and public prayer, as well as for a combination in the liturgy of the Word of the spoken and heard word.

(b) After the Gospel comes the *homily*, or what might be termed the breaking of the bread of the Word. It comes from the Greek word meaning a familiar conversation.[8] After the homilist and people have listened to the Word of God, the Homilist speaks to the congregation about the particular Scripture passages they have just heard. He doesn't replace God's Word with his own but helps the people by his commentary to be more open to the action of God's Word in their lives. He shares with them as well his own personal testimony and living of the faith.

The role of homilist traditionally belongs to the bishop or priest, and the reform of Vatican II has rightfully restored it to its proper place in the liturgy. Previously the priest removed his maniple and sometimes even his chasuble during the homily.[9] Now its connection with the rest of the Mass has been strengthened by insistence that the homily relate intimately to the Scripture and the liturgical texts of the day. It is not, however, a mere repetition of the readings but a proclamation of what these mean for the salvation of all present. As a commentary, it should inspire and exhort people to put Scripture into practice. It should also relate those particular passages to the whole of the Bible and salvation history, and especially to the concrete circumstances of that particular congregation. This demands of the homilist not only a sound knowledge of Scripture and its relationship to the liturgy but a similar insight into his people, their culture, current ideas, the events of the world, the history of the Church and its particular manifestation in the community of the priest and his congregation. The words of the New Testament were first a preached and lived reality before being written down, and this same spirit must mark the homily. This new or rather renewed emphasis of Vatican II goes far in countering the unjust accusation against Catholics that the Mass and other sacraments are quasi-magical rites that need only be seen and not understood.

(c) The *Nicene Creed* follows the homily and brings to an end a process that has been going on since the beginning of the Liturgy of the Word: God has been speaking, and the celebrant and congregation have been responding to God in various ways, and now together they sum up this response by a solemn commitment of faith.[10] This profession of faith was composed by the Council of Constantinople in 381, and it must be understood against the background of the bitter controversy that the Christian Arius began in the fourth century when he denied the divinity of Jesus. Today this creed reminds the Christian of the close connection of the Eucharist with the Sacrament of Baptism, since once the catechumens had received Baptism and were thus able to fully profess the Faith of Christ, they were not obliged to leave the Mass after this point but could instead remain for the Liturgy of the Eucharist. Pope Benedict XIV in 1014 officially inserted the Nicene Creed into its present position in the Roman Mass, but as early as 794 in the context of the Adoptionism controversy (a heresy regarding Jesus as simply a human being, in a special manner possessed of the divine spirit and "adopted" by God as His Son) it had been inserted by Charlemagne, Alcuin and Paul of Aquila in the Masses that came under their jurisdiction. The western Mozarabic rite positions the Creed immediately before Communion, and this is the more ancient practice.[11] The Nicene Creed is particularly striking when sung in some simple mode in Latin or the vernacular by celebrant and congregation together.

(d) *The General Intercessions or Common Prayer of the Faithful,* which was restored to its original position by the Second Vatican Council, traditionally brings to a close the Liturgy of the Word and most fittingly seals this first principal part of the Mass with a prayer involving the whole congregation. The ancient origin of this prayer is attested by Justin in the second century when he writes that after the readings and homily "we all rise together and offer up our prayers."[12] Although it survived down to the present day in one form or another — most vividly in the Roman liturgy on Good Friday — from the fifth century onward it fell into disuse in the Roman Rite, especially after the intercessory prayers were

added to the Roman Canon. The content of the General Intercessions is very flexible. It should include petitions for the universal and the local Church, the major concerns of the nation and
world, the suffering and the local community, but then it can
branch out to encompass the particular concerns of all those present at a particular Mass. This reveals the liturgy to be a blend of
the general and the particular, the local and universal, and that it is
not necessary that every prayer in the Mass be limited to a set pattern or formula. The celebrant introduces the General Intercessions and then concludes them with a prayer. The General
Intercessions are announced by the deacon or other minister, and
strictly speaking they are invitations to prayer rather than prayer
itself, for in that case they would be reserved to the priest.[13] The
people exercise their priestly function in this part of the Mass by
having one of their number read the Intercessions or at least by all
together responding to the petitions with an appropriate response.

B. Full participation in the Liturgy of the Word

After we have examined what constitutes a necessary prelude
to the actual celebration of the Mass in Chapters One through Five
of *A CATHOLIC BOOK OF THE MASS*, we have arrived at the first
of the two main parts of the Mass, the Liturgy of the Word. The revision of the *Roman Missal* — with all the work that went into it
— has served to restore to the Liturgy of the Word its full place in
the Mass. This involves not only a great number of specific reforms, but more importantly their ultimate aim: to emphasize,
that participation in the Liturgy of the Word is not just a matter of
the people listening to the priest or lector reading the Word, but
that this constitutes a loving encounter between God and all of His
people. It is not just a monologue on God's part, but rather a dialogue in which we respond to God not only in words but with the full
commitment of our hearts. And just as long, intimate conversations are a sign and builder of deep and lasting friendships, so too
our continued and full participation in the Mass's Liturgy of the
Word serves to strengthen our relationship with Jesus, the Word,
and through Him with His Father and Holy Spirit. In effect, we can
now sit down at the Table of the Divine Family and enter into their
loving exchange of life and love. And the response that is required
of us at Mass doesn't cease once the Mass has ended; rather, it

must continue to be made throughout the rest of the time between Masses, where the Word we have heard will become flesh in our lives. Thus, the Church at Vatican II made great progress in restoring to both celebrant and laity their proper roles in the Mass, and to all alike it has more fully opened the treasure of God's Word, both as a value in itself and as a preparation for what is to follow in the Liturgy of the Eucharist.

Chapter Six: Discussion Questions

1. Why is Vatican II's new emphasis on Scripture so important for the reform of the Liturgy of the Word?

2. Why is the Sunday Mass so important in the liturgical life of the Catholic?

3. How does it affect your attitude toward the Mass to know that the Liturgy of the Word has such strong roots in Jewish liturgical tradition?

4. What is the purpose of the introductory rites of the Mass?

5. How is the Penitential Rite of the Mass related to the Sacrament of Reconciliation?

6. How does the Mass allow for and even demand the creativity and spontaneity of both celebrant and faithful?

7. Is it unsettling for you to learn that aspects of the Mass were borrowed from the Roman world as well as from the Jewish?

8. Why is the homily so important to both the Liturgy of the Word and to the whole of the Mass?

9. Discuss how the Liturgy of the Word demands participation by both celebrant and congregation.

10. How can it be said that the liturgical reform of Vatican II restored the Liturgy of the Word to its rightful position as the first of the two parts of the Eucharistic liturgy?

CHAPTER SEVEN

Full Participation in the Liturgy of the Eucharist

> That sound tradition may be retained, and yet, the way be open for legitimate progress, a careful investigation is always to be made into each part of the liturgy which is to be revised (SC n. 23).

VII. The liturgy of the Eucharist and Vatican II

In the Dominican convent of San Marco in Florence, there is a fresco of Jesus at the Last Supper in which He is about to place the Sacred Host on the tongues of the apostles. Historically, of course, this is inaccurate, since Jesus and His apostles celebrated the first Eucharist in the context of the Jewish Passover meal and they used the customary bread of the time. It was only after nearly a thousand years that the Church adopted the use of the small white hosts for Holy Communion and the practice of placing it on the tongue of the communicant.

History aside, however, the artistic merit of this Renaissance painting is undeniable, and even more importantly it is a great testimony to the enduring faith of the Church in the Eucharist — that Jesus was as present to the 15th century when the faithful received the consecrated Bread and Wine as He was to the apostles when he shared the very same reality of Himself with them at the Last Supper. Yet, from what has been said in the previous articles concerning the scriptural, historical, theological and liturgical roots of the Mass, that age somewhat lost sight of the fuller context in which the Eucharist and particularly the Real Presence must be situated. For the Eucharist is not primarily an object of worship but an action of worship.[1] Rather than being a drama of salvation that people watch, it is a celebration in which they take part.

The second Vatican Council has reaffirmed the totality of the Church's faith in the Mass, but has done so by placing it in its full context of the Church as the "visible sacrament of saving unity" (*Lumen Gentium* n. 9), which itself more basically depends upon its intimate relationship with Jesus Christ, who has been called the first or primal sacrament, because all power in the Church flows through Him. Although the Mass is the preeminent act of worship of the Church and of the sanctification of the faithful, it too must be situated within the full public and official worship of the Church. Finally, the Mass itself must be appreciated in its composition, which includes the Liturgy of the Word as well as that of the Eucharist. Furthermore, the reforms of Vatican II allowed for the fuller participation of all the faithful in the liturgy and thus broadened it from a rather clerical preserve. It promoted "full and active participation by all the people" (*Sacrosanctum Concilium* n. 14) in a number of ways, including a preference for the communal celebration of a liturgical rite whenever possible, wider use of the vernacular, the simplification of some rites and the restoration of others such as the prayer of the faithful. This reform affected the liturgy of the Eucharist as well as the liturgy of the Word.

Christ instituted the memorial of His death and resurrection at the Last Supper. This is continually made present in the Church when the priest, acting in the person of Christ the Head (PO n. 2) carries out what the Lord commanded, for having Himself celebrated the Paschal meal and sacrifice, Jesus handed it on to His disciples to do in His memory (SC n. 47). Accordingly the Church has arranged the celebration of the Mass around the words and actions of Jesus at the Last Supper as they have been handed down in Scripture (Matthew, Mark, Luke; Paul in 1 Corinthians 11). Since Jesus celebrated the first Eucharist in the context of the Passover meal, this meal character provides the essential sacramental symbolism of the Liturgy of the Eucharist. The Missal of 1970 further clarified what has always been the basic threefold structure of this second principal part of the Mass: A., The *Preparation of the Gifts*, the setting of the table with the bread and water and wine; B., The *Eucharistic Prayer*, a hymn of thanksgiving to the Father for the whole work of salvation, especially for the sacrifice of

Christ which becomes sacramentally present again through the blessing of the bread and wine in the words of Jesus at the Last Supper (this prayer of blessing and thanksgiving was central to the Jewish Passover meal and remains so in the Christian Eucharist); and C., the *Breaking of the Bread* and *Communion*, where the one Body of Christ is shared by all the faithful and they become more fully joined through the work of the Holy Spirit. Here the meal reaches its natural climax with the distribution and the eating of the Food.

The same principles of reform employed for the Liturgy of the Word's revision were utilized for the reform of the Liturgy of the Eucharist, and this revision of the Mass more clearly reveals that the Eucharist is both a word-prayer and an action-prayer. This was principally effected by once again praying the Eucharistic Prayer or Canon aloud. This goes far toward restoring the meal dimension of the Mass, with its natural and supernatural element of dialogue and communication rather than a misleading emphasis upon mystery through silence. The restoration of the Eucharistic Prayer to its more ancient manner of celebration also underscores its basically communitarian dimension and allows this central mystery of practice and faith in the Church to be made more visible to all men and women, who then might be more easily drawn to understand and even become part of it as Catholics.

A. The Preparation of the Gifts.

This change of name from the traditional "offertory" underlines that at this point in the Mass the bread and wine are only prepared in view of the real offering that occurs in the Eucharistic Prayer. This rite consists of a twofold preparation: the bread and wine and water, the materials of the sacrifice, are brought to the altar and those present at the Mass also are reminded by the gifts that they too must make of their own lives a self-offering along with that of Christ. The restoration of the offertory procession, the second main procession of the Mass, is a great sign uniting these two dimensions, since in the present liturgy the faithful can carry up the gifts to the altar. This harks back to more ancient practice when the people actually brought the material offerings from their common stock at home to be used at the Mass. This procession, with its accompanying chant or song, dates back to the early

Church. In the Roman Mass it was a somewhat simple and practical rite, whereas in Gaul and in the Eastern rites it was a much more elaborate ritual. In the early Church bread and wine were the staples of an agrarian economy, and so there was a more significant link between the Mass and daily life, further intensified by the bread's having the appearance of ordinary bread. The offertory procession, while not just involving the laity, was a rite strictly reserved to the baptized and so can be seen as a solemn ritual exercise of the priesthood of the baptized faithful. Accordingly, Vatican II restored to the laity their rightful place in this procession.

1. In line with these general rules and the nature of the rite of the preparation of the gifts, *the offertory procession,* as one of the important elements of the liturgy of the Eucharist, should be so carried out with due solemnity that its purpose is clear: the gifts of bread and wine offered by the faithful should appear inseparable from their final sacrificial destination and a prelude to their reception in Communion. The faithful approach with the bread and wine; the celebrant pronounces over them the words of Consecration, and the faithful again approach in the communion procession to receive the Body of Christ. It is part of the exercise of the baptismal priesthood to bring the gifts to the altar, which the priest then offers up as an exercise of his ministerial priesthood. Thus, in this one rite, properly observed, the one Priesthood of Christ is shown in its diversity and unity. St. Augustine put this in its fullest perspective when he said: "Just as the priest receives from you that which he offers for you, so our Priest receives from us that which He offers up for us: the flesh in which He was sacrificed."[3] This reveals the deepest spiritual and doctrinal dimensions of the offertory rite, which is much more than a mere practical gesture.

Never, of course, must it be assumed that we are giving anything to God which He has not first given to us. His love alone makes the Mass possible. And these gifts are but a slight return for His goodness to each of the faithful. We plead also that He continue His saving work among His unworthy people by particularly joining these gifts to the perfect sacrifice of His Son.

In time the practice and the meaning of the offertory procession were greatly eclipsed, and it was reduced to a ritualized collection of money, which appeared to have little to do with the bread and wine. The practice of the collection for the poor, however, goes back to St. Paul and his begging of a collection for the Church at Jerusalem. Likewise, from the very nature of the Mass as an offering by Christ for all men and women, a collection is not at all out of place. In the early Church as well, much more bread and wine was offered than was actually consecrated and the surplus was distributed in part to the needy. Thus the present offertory procession rightfully encompasses both kinds of offerings.

The Mass stipend — an offering made that a special intention be remembered at a particular Mass — marks the final form of evolution of this procession.[4] Although this custom remains valid today, a stipend never buys exclusive rights to any Mass or, for that matter, to any spiritual or graced reality in the Church. For every Mass has the intention and efficacy of the salvation of all the world. Also, this special kind of offering acquires its fullest meaning when those who request the Mass both attend and particpate in that particular celebration. Historically, the importance of the offertory procession declined as the reception of Communion by the faithful became less frequent. One great factor in its decline occurred in the 11th century when the original loaves of bread used in the Mass were replaced by the small hosts of unleavened bread with which we are still familiar today.

2. After the minister or server has placed the corporal, purificator, chalice and missal on the altar and the priest has received the gifts, *the priest individually raises the bread and wine* to the accompaniment of prayers which were inspired by the Jewish mealtime liturgy. The mixing of wine and water is an ancient custom and is linked to the two natures in the one Person of Christ and to the blood and water flowing from the wounded side of Christ on the cross. The gifts may be incensed, and this is the most ancient and important of the various incensations in the Mass in the Roman rite. The priest's washing of hands in the Gallican and Eastern rites has a symbolic sense of purification, and this meaning is also valid for the Roman tradition. However, the Roman mentality would generally view such an action as primarily functional, a necessity imposed by the handling of a substantial amount of offertory gifts.

3. The *Pray, Brethren* or *Orate, frates* originated in the land of Charlemagne, in Gaul, and was originally addressed to the priests who surrounded the celebrant. Later, at low Masses, it was

addressed to the congregation, and before the present response was selected, it was chiefly understood as an invitation to silent prayer.

4. The *Prayer over the gifts* or *Secret* is the only prayer of the priest in this part of the Mass that comes from the Roman tradition strictly speaking.[6] It is essentially a very concise prayer, variable in content, and thus resembles the Opening and Postcommunion prayers. In an abbreviated fashion it contains the themes of the offering that will later be developed in the Eucharistic Prayer.

B. The Eucharistic Prayer

Just as there are a variety of terms to describe the one saving reality which the Church calls Mass — Eucharist, liturgy, the Lord's Supper, to mention a few — so too are there several terms to describe this second part of the liturgy of the Eucharist. The term *Eucharistic Prayer* is found in the Missal of 1970 and replaces the older designation *canon*, which implies something that is standard in form and content. The more eastern usage of *anaphora* is similar to the meaning of canon but only less so because it implies a more limited amount of standardization.[7]

Actually the designation of the term canon to the Eucharistic Prayer was not accurate until three or four centuries into the Church's existence. This title, strictly speaking, refers precisely to the opening dialogue of the Eucharistic Prayer: *The Lord be with you. And also with you. Lift up your hearts. We lift them up to the Lord. Let us give thanks to the Lord our God. It is right to give Him thanks and praise.* For many centuries the few essential elements of the Preface and Eucharistic Prayer were subject to improvisation on the part of the celebrant. These essential elements of the Eucharistic Prayer are: 1., Thanksgiving, initiated in the Preface but carried throughout the whole Prayer; 2., Sanctus, which divides what was the complete unity of Preface and Eucharistic Prayer; 3., Epiclesis, the invocation of the Holy Spirit upon the bread and wine and upon the faithful who receive them; 4., Institution Narrative or words of Consecration; 5. Anamnesis — memorial words of both priest and people — following the words of Institution; 6. Offering of the bread and wine to the Father through the Son in the Holy Spirit; 7. Intercessions for the living and dead; and 8. the Final Doxology with the Great Amen.[8]

Early in the history of the Church in the East, the Eucharistic Prayers were set in a fixed pattern. Great saints such as John Chrysostom were responsible for this, and today these prayers still bear their names. In the West by comparison there was a much longer period of improvisation and variability. The various essential elements of the Eucharistic Prayer long remained independent of one another, but they tended to be unified around such as the particular theme at that point in the Church's liturgical year. In the Roman rite the Preface continued to vary with the season, or particular feasts, even when the Eucharistic Prayer truly became a Canon and was permanently fixed. The Roman Canon or Eucharistic Prayer I, as it is now officially designated in the Missal of 1970, is almost exactly the same as it was at the time of Pope Gregory the Great at the turn of the sixth century. It had a long and complex development, but the history of this is mostly lost to us today.[9] The principal author was probably Pope St. Damasus I (366-384), and it reflects a Latin rather than a Greek origin, for it has a biblical style but is marked by the rhythm and vocabulary of Roman discourse. In the fourth century its use was imposed on all the churches in Rome and throughout Italy.

In the present Missal there has been something of a return to the practice of the earlier Church with the addition of three new Eucharistic Prayers, although in each of these the words of Institution are the same. In each of them the role of the Holy Spirit is given greater emphasis than is apparent in the Roman Canon. This follows the tradition of the Eastern churches where the theology of the Holy Spirit knew a golden age only after the definitive formation of the Roman Canon.[10] Now there is included in all three Prayers an epiclesis or invocation of the Holy Spirit, prayed over both the gifts of bread and wine (before the words of Institution) and over the faithful, that they may be unified by these gifts of the Body and Blood of Christ (after the words of Institution).

The memorial dimension of the Mass is pivotal, since Christ said *Do this in memory of me.* Thus, the actual Consecration of the Mass and indeed the whole Mass is the anamnesis. But, specifically, the celebrant and the people have their own anamnesis in the Mass. For the people this is the memorial acclamation (e.g.,

Christ has died, Christ is risen, Christ will come again), introduced by the *Mystery of faith*, which in turn was formerly contained in the words of consecration over the wine. The priest's anamnesis follows this when he recalls Our Lord's "death, his descent among the dead, his resurrection, and his ascension to your right hand; and, looking forward to his coming in glory, we offer you his body and blood, the acceptable sacrifice which brings salvation to the whole world" (Eucharistic Prayer IV).

Each of these prayers has a particular suitability: *I* is most appropriately prayed on Sundays, feasts of the apostles and of other saints named within it; *II* is largely derived from the most ancient text of the Mass — from the *Apostolic Constitution* of Hippolytus (third century) — with its own Preface (recalling that the Preface and the Eucharistic Prayer formed a unity before the introduction of the Sanctus) and is more suitable for weekdays; *III* has the use of a variable Preface in accordance with the Roman tradition and can be used on Sundays and feast days instead of *I*; *IV* derives from Syrian liturgies and contains many biblical allusions, especially from St. John, as well as its own Preface, which joins the whole of the prayer to give a very comprehensive picture of all the Christian mysteries.[11]

1. Returning to elements common to all the Eucharistic Prayers, it will be recalled from above that the *opening dialogue prior to the Preface* was originally the only fixed part of all the elements which together became the Canon of the Mass. This dialogue is present in all Christian liturgies from the beginning of the third century. It begins the Eucharistic Prayer with a dialogic character that will also mark its close with the Great Amen. Among its other dimensions, it serves to emphasize the essential involvement of the faithful in this sacrifice of praise which is the Mass.

2. *The Preface* invariably opens as a prayer of thanksgiving to God. In this sense it is an initial proclamation of what will be the resounding theme of gratitude that gives the name "Eucharist" ("Thanksgiving" in Greek) to the Mass. It is a prayer addressed to the Father in thanksgiving for the redemption being carried on in the Mass. It usually centers on the Person of Christ but varies with the liturgical season, feasts, and particular occasions of many types. The whole Church, in the person of the priest, gives thanks that she is made part of the prayer and sacrifice of Christ through the gift of the Spirit to the Father, a renewal of her covenant with God and of her bridegroom relationship with Christ. This emphasis upon thanksgiving comes originally from the Passover meal that Jesus celebrated with His disciples at the Last Supper. It contained two blessings. One was pronounced over the bread and the other over the cup. In time the second and longer blessing over the cup came to include the first in one prayer of thanksgiving. Thus did the Mass begin in the context of the Jewish table blessing, although all the elements have been completely transformed by Jesus. In keeping with the Roman tradition of variable Prefaces, 80 new ones have been added to the Mass by the Missal of 1970.

3. The Preface concludes with the *Sanctus* or *Holy, Holy, Holy*. This originated in the East and only came to the West in the fourth century. It derives from Isaiah 6:3 and also bears comparison with Daniel 7:9ff. Although it interrupts what was once a complete unity of Preface and Eucharistic Prayer, it most appropriately brings out the nature of the Mass as a sacrifice of praise, whose effect is further heightened by being recited or sung by both celebrant and congregation.

4. In the Roman Rite the *words of Institution or Consecration* are viewed as bringing about the transformation of the bread and wine into the Body and Blood of Christ, while in the Eastern churches this role is attributed to the epiclesis, the invocation of the Holy Spirit upon the gifts of bread and wine.[12] Historically, the Roman tradition seems to be more ancient, for in the third century Mass text (the oldest we have) furnished us by Hippolytus, the epiclesis has no consecratory function.[13] The Eastern tradition arose with the great development of the theology of the Holy Spirit among the Greek Fathers, such as Cyril of Jerusalem in the fourth century. It was only in the 14th century, however, that bitter controversy arose over this point, since up to this time there was no strict emphasis upon the exact moment of the transformation.

In the Roman Canon there seems never to have been an epiclesis with the power of consecration attributed to it. Yet, just before the Words of Institution, there is an emphasis upon the symbolic and sacramental nature of the offerings,[14] and this prayer begs the Father to give them their full spiritual character: "an offering in spirit and in truth." In the Roman Canon there is also another prayer similar to the epiclesis which asks the Father to accept this earthly sacrifice at His altar in heaven — a sacrifice that will enable the worshipers to receive the Body and Blood of Jesus and be filled with every grace and blessing. This also appears to be the more primitive formulation — the invocation or prayer for unity in the Holy Spirit — and is linked to a plea that the faithful who receive Communion may be united more fully and filled with all blessings. The most ancient Mass text — on which Eucharistic Prayer II is based — also agrees with this manner of formulation. This style of prayer addressed to the Holy Spirit is the model for the new Eucharistic Prayers as well. Although the practice of the Roman rite seems to be the more ancient in this regard, it is beneficial for the Western Church to have the presence of these special prayers to the Holy Spirit in the Mass, for they bring to the West more of the riches of the Eastern branch of the Church.

The Institution narrative, or words of Consecration over the bread and wine, represents the climax of the whole Eucharistic Prayer and indeed the whole Mass. It forms the heart of every known Eucharistic Prayer, with the possible exception of two.[15] This is the actual anamnesis or memorial reenactment of Christ's command, *Do this in memory of me.* Here the Church is visibly carrying out what Christ instructed at the Last Supper. This is the precise reason why the words are effective and bring about the transformation of the bread and wine into the Body and Blood of Christ. The four Eucharistic Prayers give the same wording to the Institution narrative, although there are differences among Matthew, Mark, Luke and 1 Corinthians 11, and although there are more than 80 liturgical versions of the Institution narrative varying in greater or lesser degree from one another. Accordingly, throughout the history of the Mass, there has been a concern for tradition but not for literal exactitude.[16] Based on very sound theology, the Eucharistic Prayers add to the words of Consecration over the cup "the blood of the new and everlasting covenant." This underscores the eschatological dimension of the Eucharist brought out most forcefully in the Institution narrative of Matthew: *"I shall not drink wine until the day I drink the new wine with you in the kingdom of my Father"* (26:29).

At present the priest elevates the Precious Body and Blood after each has been consecrated and then genuflects as well. This came about only in the medieval period as a result of controversies about the Eucharist during the 12th and 13th centuries. There was a great popular demand to see the Consecrated Body of the Lord, but unfortunately this served to replace more frequent reception of Holy Communion. It can't be lost sight of that the Institution narrative is part of a greater whole: the Eucharistic prayer-action is part of a continuous unity extending from the preparation of the gifts to the reception of these same gifts after they have been consecrated.

5. The phrase *Mystery of Faith* has been taken from its former place in the words of consecration over the cup and now introduces the anamnesis or memorial acclamation of the congregation. This emphasizes more fully the integral part of the faithful in celebrating along with the priest this central commemorative rite of Jesus' death, resurrection and promise of future coming in glory — especially as it is situated between the Institution narrative and the anamnesis of the priest. Yet, in his anamnesis, the priest joins himself with the rest of the Church in recalling these sacred mysteries which enable this offering to be transformed into the "bread of life and the cup of eternal salvation." Recalling what was said above about the epiclesis, we find the Holy Spirit again directly invoked at this point in the Mass in Eucharistic Prayers II, III, and IV, that He might bring together in unity all those who are to partake of these transformed offerings. In this way the role of every member of the Trinity is emphasized at this climactic point of the Mass. In all known liturgies, the words of Institution and the anamnesis are very closely linked.

6. The Roman Canon is very rich in *intercessory prayers* both before and after the Consecration. Before the Consecration come intercessions for the local and universal Church and for all the living. This represents a strong affirmation of the bond of the Communion of Saints and of the intercessory powers of the saints as well. Along with the liturgical tradition of Alexandria (which with Antioch and Rome made up the three great liturgical centers of the early Church), the Roman Canon places intercessions in immediate connection with the opening of the Eucharistic Prayer, emphasizing praise and thanksgiving, while the three new Eucharistic Prayers place the intercessions near the end of the Prayer, a practice in keeping with the tradition of Antioch. No matter what their position, however, the presence of such intercessions manifests the belief of the Church that intercessions presented during the course of the Mass are of special weight. It is also noteworthy that the Roman Canon allows for the naming of particular members of the faithful, both living and dead, and Eucharistic Prayers II and III have a special commemoration for the dead — that of III being particularly eloquent about the meaning of death for the Christian.

7. *The doxology and the great Amen* close the Eucharistic Prayer. The doxology is a crystallization of theological reflection on the Trinity, and the gesture of raising the Body and Blood of Christ high above the altar is most expressive of what has just been accomplished. The great Amen of the congregation not only expresses their faith in what has just happened but includes as well their participation in this action of offering the sacrifice of Christ along with the priest. For this reason it is the most important of the faithful's acclamations and so brings to a close in dialogue the Prayer that was opened in the very same fashion. Of interest historically is that the words before the doxology in the Roman Canon are a remnant of the days when different kinds of earthly goods were blessed at this point in the Mass. For instance, new beans were blessed on the Ascension,[17] but in the Roman liturgy there was strict control over the number of offerings allowed on the altar.

C. Communion rite

1. The recitation or singing of the *Our Father* opens the third part of the liturgy of the Eucharist, the rite of Communion. Although the Communion of the faithful isn't essential for the validity of the Mass, it certainly is necessary for its integrity.[18] While the Our Father was of general importance in the spiritual and doctrinal life of the early Church, and wasn't confined to the Mass, at least from the fourth century it has traditionally been seen as a preparation for Communion. This was so because of the prayer's fourth petition, "Give us this day our daily bread," which we understood as referring to the Eucharistic Body of Christ. It was likewise based on the belief that God wouldn't accept the offering of those who hadn't been reconciled to their brothers and sisters — and the Our Father's linking of forgiveness of sins by God and mutual forgiveness among men and women represented for the Christians an immediate purification before Communion. At first the Our Father was reserved to the celebrant, thus emphasizing its nature as a priestly prayer, but the Missal of 1970 follows the Eastern Church usage, where it is recited or sung by priest and congregation together. In the Roman Mass the Our Father was first placed after the breaking of the bread, but Pope Gregory the Great moved it to its present position, judging that it should be closer to the words of Institution because it likewise was given directly by Christ.

2. The rite of the *Kiss (or Sign) of Peace* dates back to St. Justin in the second century, and its original position was immediately before the offertory, after the prayers of the faithful. This gives concrete form to the injunction in the Gospel of Matthew that brothers or sisters at enmity should first be reconciled before presenting their gifts at the altar. Now it is viewed as a very natural and profitable extension of the Lord's Prayer leading into Communion. It is at heart not just a greeting or welcome but a prayer which should be a very personal and sincere promise of reconciliation and peace in view of Communion and the first words of the Risen Jesus to His apostles: *Peace be with you.* Furthermore, the Kiss of Peace is not reserved to the celebrant. The celebrant, by gesture and greeting, gives the Sign of Peace to the whole community, and they then exchange it with one another. Perhaps the change in position in the Mass might have taken place to preserve the Sign of Peace for those who were intending to stay for Communion, since those who did not have this intention might have departed before the Communion Rite. In the Roman Rite, however, the Mass was normally seen as concluded only after the postcommunion prayer.

3. *The fraction* or the *breaking of the (consecrated) Bread* occurs very quickly in the present celebration of the Mass, but this was not the case when ordinary bread was used. It was always seen as having a great symbolic value, for it was done by Christ Himself and "breaking of the bread" was held as so characteristic of the Eucharist that it became a synonym for it, as in Luke 24:30-35 and Acts 2:42. It was viewed as the great sign and source of unity, of the many united in the one Body of Christ. The present rite asks that the priest consecrate a host large enough to be broken into a number of pieces, some of which may be given to at least a few of the faithful for their Communion. Originally this took place before the Our Father, until Pope Gregory the Great changed the practice, but for many centuries before Vatican II it had quietly been done during the conclusion of the "Lord, deliver us" prayer following the Our Father. With the restoration of this rite, the connection between the sign of peace and the fraction and Communion is highlighted. The fraction can be seen not just as a practical function — although it is this — but as a prayer for peace and the unity of the Church and of all mankind. It is especially a sign of the mutual love — in the face of any kind of disunity — that should already exist among the assembled congregation, love that should increase and be strengthened when they receive the Body and Blood of Christ at Communion.

After the fraction, the celebrant puts a piece of the Consecrated Host into the chalice. Among other beliefs, the fourth-century Syrians saw this action as a kind of reenactment of the resurrection of Jesus upon the altar and as a symbolic reunion of what had apparently been separated and destroyed in the sacrifice. This comingling can also be seen as a sign of the anticipated Communion of all the faithful in view of their resurrection. In Rome the Pope would send one of the particles from his Host to each of the priests of the Roman churches where they were celebrating Mass for their people, and every priest would drop this particle into his chalice as a sign of unity between the bishop and all of his priests and flock.

4. The *Lamb of God* or *Agnus Dei* was the first real penitential rite of the Mass, and it was situated in its present position in the Mass by Pope Sergius I (687-701). It was meant to accompany the rather long rite of the breaking of the Consecrated Bread when loaves of bread were still used. Accordingly, although the Kiss of Peace came after the liturgy of the Word in the early Church, the present rite emphasizes how penance leads into the rite of peace and then ultimately to Communion.

5. Even from the time of Augustine in the fifth century, there is evidence that frequent *Communion* had already begun to decline. Those who intended to depart early were sent off with a blessing, which Augustine attests took place after the Our Father but before Communion and was seen as a sort of substitute — albeit a very weak one — for the preeminent blessing of the reception of the Body and Blood of Christ. In the Church in Gaul these blessings became quite elaborate and solemn. In Rome, however, the normal departure came only after the postcommunion prayer, and Pope Zachary in the eighth century even spoke out against this early departure as contrary to the tradition of the apostles. Apparently, however, this didn't stop its continuing and spreading during the Middle Ages.[19]

The Communion rite has been revised by the Second Vatican Council to bring out its integral nature in the full context of the Mass. First the priest invites the congregation to receive the Body and Blood of Christ by use of the biblically based formula *Behold the Lamb of God*, whose first part is based on John 1:29 while the second part is based on Revelation 19:9. The response is based on Matthew 8:8. This is a sign of the unity of the Communion rite between priest and people. The celebrant then partakes of the Body and Blood of Christ, and after him all the clergy by rank. The priest, as a private preparation, prays silently either one of two prayers provided in the Missal. Before communicating he says *May the Body (Blood) of Christ bring me to everlasting life. Amen.* When distributing Communion to the people, he uses the very simple but ancient formula *Body (Blood) of Christ.* The equally simple response of *Amen* by the faithful nonetheless involves them individually in a personal act of faith. The people may either stand or kneel to receive Communion, although standing is the more ancient custom and has been so retained in the Eastern churches. To accompany the Communion procession, the third and final great procession of the Mass along with those of the entrance and offertory, a communion chant or song is recited or sung. Psalm 34 has been a traditional chant from the fourth and fifth centuries.

In the ancient Church, the faithful always received both the Host and the Precious Blood, and this has continued in the Eastern Churches. In the West this continued up until the 13th century, although drinking from the chalice for the celebrant is still considered indispensable for the validity of the Mass. For both celebrant and faithful, there have been many ways to receive the Precious Blood — drinking from the chalice itself, taking it with a spoon or straw or by dipping the Host into the chalice (intinction). Yet, even in ancient times, only the Host was taken to the sick or absent. The Council of Trent, in the face of attacks by reformers who wished to return the cup to the faithful, explained in light of the Church's faith that the entire Jesus is present in each of the species taken separately. Vatican II has allowed for Communion under both species in certain circumstances.

The restoration of the cup to the faithful serves to emphasize more fully the sign value of the Mass, which speaks of the unity of the one bread and the one cup. It also adds to the eschatological dimension of the Mass, to the "relation of the Eucharistic banquet to the heavenly banquet," as the General Instruction to the Mass states it (GI n. 240). Jesus Himself gives it this aspect in the Gospel of Matthew: "I shall not drink wine until the day I drink the new wine with you in the kingdom of my Father" (26:29). The description of the Father's kingdom as a banquet, used by Jesus several times, is a theme from the Old Testament. St. Thomas Aquinas brings out this eschatological dimension of the Eucharist when he speaks of it as our pledge of future glory. For indeed the Church is the beginning of the Kingdom, and it is through the celebration of the Eucharist by the community of Christ in the Church that we shall come to celebrate the eternal banquet in heaven. The Eucharist is the sacrament of hope as well as of faith and love.

The sacramental and sign value of the bread was also the object of revision by the Second Vatican Council. The General Instruction to the Mass notes that the sign demands that the material for the Eucharistic celebration appear as actual food (GI n. 283), and the Missal states that at least some of the people should be able to partake of Communion broken from the very Host of the celebrant. These instructions go far toward restoring the meaning of the fraction or breaking of the Bread and the meaning of Communion as an integral part of the Mass. This had been diminished somewhat, from the 18th century on, when the faithful at Mass received Holy Communion that had been consecrated at a previous Mass and then placed in the tabernacle. This represents an interruption in what should be the unity of Consecration and Communion, although of course, with large numbers of faithful present at Mass, it is almost unavoidable to have recourse to this in some cases. However, the norm — in conformity with the Missal of 1570 as well as that of 1970 — is that the bread destined for Communion at a particular Mass should be consecrated at that Mass. This reemphasis on the sign value of the Communion rite and its elements, which can never be separated from the basic nature of the sacraments, also underlines the connection of the Offertory and Communion processions and their meaning. For the very gifts that the faithful, as part of the dignity and function of their baptismal priesthood, have presented to the priest in the Offertory procession — which in the past they brought directly from their homes — are the same they receive back after they have been transformed in the Eucharistic Prayer. All in all, the revision of Vatican II and its continuing pronouncements on the liturgy have greatly advanced the ancient tradition of the Church: that for both clergy and laity the reception of the Body and Blood at Mass is a normal part of the liturgy and only serious sin should keep one from it.

6. With the conclusion of the rite of Communion a hymn or song of praise may be sung, but the faithful can as profitably be left to private meditation on the Sacrament they have just received. In this way, just as with the opening prayer and the prayer over the gifts, the celebrant's *postcommunion prayer* may become a kind of summation of all these personal prayers of the faithful. In structure and function and history, the postcommunion prayer, a prayer of thanksgiving adapted to the season or feast day, is related to the opening and offertory prayers. It has been the normal conclusion to the Mass since the time of Gregory the Great.

7. The actual *conclusion* of the Mass in the Roman rite, just like its beginning, has always been traditionally abrupt. It includes a *greeting* by the celebrant, his *blessing* and the actual *dismissal*, in Latin, *Ite, missa est*, which gave the Eucharist in the West its traditional name of "Mass." This formula of dismissal is very ancient and meaningful in the context of the Roman Mass. For, now that the faithful have been enriched by God's Word and the Body and Blood of the Lord and strengthened in the unity of the Holy Spirit, they can return to their daily lives to do God's will and show His love in all they do and to all they meet. The Missal of 1970 allows for a greater variety of blessings and for more elaborate forms of them. These serve to underline that the Sacrifice and Sacrament of the eating and drinking of the Body and Blood of Jesus are the supreme blessing in the life of the Christian, a blessing whose fruits the Christian should take along from the Mass and which should serve to transform the world in which he or she lives.

Also, just as the revision of Vatican II removed the priest's private prayers from the beginning of the Mass, so too at the end the reading of the prologue to the Gospel of St. John was removed from the text of the Mass. Traditionally it was also seen as a kind of blessing.

D. Full participation in the Liturgy of the Eucharist

The Mass reaches its climax in the Liturgy of the Eucharist. The loving conversation that was carried on during the Liturgy of the Word leads naturally into the most intimate union with the Body and Blood of Jesus — for each individual Catholic and for the Church as a whole. This unity with our Lord and Savior doesn't occur on just the physical or spiritual level of our existence, but it is a total union. The best image to describe it is that of the love between husband and wife, an image that both the Old and New Testaments use to describe our relationship with God (cf. the Book of Hosea and Paul's Letter to the Ephesians, ch. 5). God alone can initiate this intimate relationship, but it will never reach its full potential unless each of us responds with the whole of our person and with complete love. Thus, all the dimensions of participation in the Mass that have been discussed so far find their ultimate basis and motivation in the love that God shows and shares with us, especially in the Eucharist. And just as God is fully present to us in the Mass and throughout the rest of our lives, so too are we invited and challenged to be equally present to God and one another — both at Mass and throughout the rest of our lives, which should be a mirror image of what we profess and do at Mass. The beauty and urgency of this call are expressed by the Letter to the Hebrews:

> *Let us keep firm in the hope we profess, because the one who made the promise is faithful. Let us be concerned for each other, to stir a response in love and good works. Do not stay away from the assemblies of the community, as some do, but encourage each other to go; the more so as you see the Day drawing near* (Hebrews 10:23-25).

Chapter Seven: Discussion Questions

1. Discuss how the same principles of reform have been applied to both the Liturgy of the Word and the Liturgy of the Eucharist.

2. What is the significance of the offering of the gifts at Mass?

3. How do the faithful as well as the celebrant participate in the Offertory Rite?

4. What do you think about the suitability of the Mass stipend?

5. Do you think that there should be an even greater variety in the number of approved Eucharistic Prayers or do you think that something valuable was lost by allowing alternatives to the Roman Canon?

6. Discuss how the Prefaces contain such succinct statements of doctrine.

7. Why is the Kiss of Peace so important to the Mass as a sign and instrument of unity?

8. Why is the reception of Holy Communion an integral part of the Mass?

9. How does reception of Holy Communion under the forms of both bread and wine contribute to the celebration of the Mass?

CHAPTER EIGHT

The Blessed Virgin Mary as the Model of Full Participation in the Mass

"At the root of the Eucharist is the virginal and maternal life of Mary" (Pope John Paul II).

VIII. The Mystery of the Eucharist and the Blessed Virgin Mary

Vatican II's *Constitution on the Sacred Liturgy* solemnly defines the liturgy — and especially the Eucharist — as "the outstanding means by which the faithful can express in their lives, and manifest to others, the mystery of Christ and the real nature of the true Church" (SC n. 2). The liturgy and Christ and the Church are intimately connected. Yet, it would be an incomplete picture without reference to the Blessed Virgin Mary. Pope John Paul II reminded us of this when he said that "at the root of the Eucharist is the virginal and maternal life of Mary."[1] For Mary was the "first redeemed"[2] and is "mother of the Church."[3] This means that Mary "had an active part"[4] in Christ's Sacrifice, that "with a motherly heart she associated herself with His Sacrifice; with love she consented to His immolation . . . she offered Him and she offered herself to the Father."[5] And so, "every Mass puts us in intimate communion with her, the mother, whose sacrifice 'becomes present' just as the Sacrifice of her Son 'becomes present' at the words of consecration of the bread and wine pronounced by the priest."[6] Thus Mary is at one and the same time in complete solidarity with all men and women, for she "prepared that Body and Blood of Jesus as a gift from the whole human family";[7] and yet intimately linked to the Trinity ("her overflowing experience of God"[8]), for she placed complete trust in God's Word: *I am the handmaid of*

the Lord . . . let what you have said be done to me (Luke
1:38), and thus through the power of the Holy Spirit and not through
human power did "her flesh"[9] become a "temple"[10] and "her
heart"[11] an "altar"[12] for the Lord.

A. The B.V.M. and her role in the plan of salvation

The words of the Pope also serve to return us to what the
Church at Vatican II solemnly proclaimed about Mary: that she
"figured profoundly in the history of salvation and in a certain way
unites and mirrors within herself the central truths of the faith"
(LG n. 65); that the "offices and privileges of the Blessed Virgin
Mary," rightly explained, "are always related to Christ, the
Source of all truth, sanctity, and piety" (LG n. 67); that the "maternal duty of Mary toward men in no way obscures or diminishes
this unique mediation of Christ, but rather shows its power" (LG n.
60; cf. n. 62); that Mary's role in the plan of salvation serves in no
way to "impede the immediate union of the faithful with Christ,"
but rather, "to foster this union" (LG n. 60); that Mary became
such a mother "by accepting God's word in faith" (LG n. 63); that
her divine maternity not only unites her to her Son in a most special
way but also intimately unites her to the Church, for

> Indeed she is "clearly the mother of the members of Christ . . .
> since she cooperated out of love so that there might be born in
> the Church the faithful, who are members of Christ their
> Head."[13] Therefore she is also hailed as a preeminent and alto-
> gether singular member of the Church, and as the Church's
> model and excellent exemplar in faith and charity. Taught by
> the Holy Spirit, the Catholic Church honors her with filial af-
> fection and piety as a most beloved mother (LG n. 53).

The Council further proclaimed that "in the bodily and spiritual
glory which she possesses in heaven, the Mother of Jesus continues
in this present world as the image and first flowering of the Church
as she is to be perfected in the world to come" (LG n. 68); that in
the "most holy Virgin the Church has already reached that perfection whereby she exists without spot or wrinkle . . ." (LG n. 65);
and finally, that "by her manifold acts of intercession Mary continues to win for us gifts of eternal salvation" (LG n. 62).

B. The B.V.M. as the model of full participation in the Mass

Thus it is on this solid basis of the Church's Faith that we must always venerate the memory of Mary (LG n. 52) and pay her special reverence (LG n. 66) and indeed if we do this "within the limits of sound and orthodox doctrine" (LG n. 66) inevitably devotion to Mary will lead us to a stronger faith in and celebration of the Eucharist. And so Mary serves to bring A CATHOLIC BOOK OF THE MASS not only to a conclusion but to something of a climax — by summing up in her own person its message, both in content and spirit, and by providing us with the perfect model of full participation in the Mystery of the Eucharist. For, following in the footsteps of her Son, she lived a full life on earth but yet lived it always in anticipation of the world to come (cf. LG n. 55). This, then, serves to put into full perspective the insistence of A CATHOLIC BOOK OF THE MASS that full participation in the Mass involves not only actual presence at the Eucharist but also fulfilling the roles of pastor, biblicist, historian, theologian and liturgist. And in Mary's life, as witnessed in Scripture, these roles are revealed not only as the product of an intellectual effort — important as this is (cf. SC n. 23) — but as the fruit of a life of faith, hope and charity such as Mary lived so fully.

Before we pass on to this presentation, however, it is important to note that Mary's position in the plan of salvation is indeed unique. For on the one hand she "occupies a place in the Church which is the highest after Christ and yet very close to us" (LG n. 53); she "was entirely holy and free from all stain of sin, fashioned by the Holy Spirit into a kind of new substance and new creature," and thus "she far surpasses all other creatures" (LG n. 56). Yet, on the other hand, Mary "belongs to the offspring of Adam, she is one with all human beings in their need for salvation" (LG n. 53), and "with a full heart . . . she devoted herself totally as a handmaid of the Lord to the person and work of her Son" (LG n. 56). Mary "cooperated by her obedience, faith, hope and burning charity. . ." (LG n. 61) with God's special grace given to her, and this she did in full freedom (LG n. 56). With this reaffirmation of Mary's special relationship with God, which at the same time didn't alter her humanity, her complete solidarity with every man and woman, it is now possible to pass on to the vision of Mary's full participation in the Mystery of the Eucharist which is revealed in Scripture.

1. Mary is revealed to us in Scripture as a model of what it means to embody the *pastoral spirit* that should characterize every Catholic's participation in the Mass. Mary's visit to Elizabeth to comfort her in her pregnancy (Luke 1) and her attendance at the wedding feast of Cana, where she prompted Jesus to work the first miracle of His public life (John 2), show how closely she followed in the footsteps of Jesus, the Good Shepherd, the Pastor (cf. John 10). At one and the same time Mary showed her complete fidelity to God — Elizabeth called her blessed because she believed *"that the promise made her by the Lord would be fulfilled"* (Luke 1:45), and she said to the wedding servants, *"Do whatever he tells you"* (John 2:6) — and yet also showed her concern to meet the needs of others, to increase their happiness, despite the inconvenience it caused her.

Mary always stayed close to Christ, and this was the source of her pastoral spirit. Likewise we must stay close to Christ, especially in the Eucharist and its fullness of belief and celebration, if we would follow in that same spirit. And so just as God showed us His infinite love by creating us and by then redeeming us in Christ, a redemption we most fully experience in the Eucharist, and just as this same pastoral love prompted the Church to reform the Mass so that it would take advantage of every divine and human resource to make it all it is supposed to be, so too this pastoral spirit should characterize our part in the Eucharist and in the life that should flow from it.

In imitation of Mary, then, this pastoral spirit is revealed as a spirit of joy, of celebration and of festivity. Accordingly, every Mass must be a worthy and fitting celebration, but it must also be joyful and festive. This means not a party atmosphere, but that each of us must respond as fully as possible to God's grace and so enter into the celebration as fully as possible, giving ourselves to it ever more completely. Thus we will more and more become a part of the Eucharist and of God's Family, and by our example will encourage others to do the same. This spirit is also one of belonging, for the Mass is not an individual act but the activity of the community. Hence each must do one's part in making everyone else feel a vital part of the Eucharistic community. This spirit is also one of anticipation, for God will become present here in a way that is nowhere else equalled. This sense of anticipation doesn't so much seek to lift us out of the routine and mundane as to allow us to see that God is present and active in every moment of our lives. Thus we should strive not so much to make the Eucharist a part of our lives as to make our lives a part of the Eucharist, which is Life (cf. John 6).

2. Mary is also revealed in Scripture as a model of what it means to embody the *biblical spirit* that should characterize every Catholic's participation in the Mass. For Mary

> received His [Jesus'] praise when, in extolling a kingdom beyond the calculations and bonds of flesh and blood, He declared blessed . . . those who heard and kept the Word of God, as she was faithfully doing . . . (LG n. 58).

In this way all of the many reforms undertaken by Vatican II regarding the Word of God have this as their aim: that each of us imitate Mary's complete faith in simply taking God at His Word, which is the model of Old and New Testament faithfulness. Often enough it is this simplicity that confounds us. This is particularly brought out in the Old Testament episode involving Naaman the Syrian, who came to Israel to be cured of his leprosy (2 Kings 5) and who at first balked at the simplicity of having to wash seven times in the River Jordan until more sensible heads prevailed:

> *"If the prophet had told you to do something extraordinary, would you not have done it? All the more now, since he said to you, 'wash and be clean,' should you do as he said"* (2 Kings 5:13-14)

And it is not only the simplicity of Mary's faith that gives us an example of how to enter most fully into the Mass, but it was her acceptance of the Word of God that enabled the Word to become flesh and dwell sacramentally in the bodies of each of us.

3. Mary is also revealed in Scripture as a model of what it means to embody the *historical and liturgical spirit* that should characterize every Catholic's participation in the Mass. This is particularly visible at the Presentation of Jesus in the Temple, where amazing prophecies were spoken about Jesus and Mary (Luke 2:21-38); at the finding of Jesus in the Temple among the doctors of the Law, when he said, *I must be about my Father's* *business* (Luke 2:41-50), and when Mary was present among the followers of Jesus "prayerfully imploring the gift of the Spirit, who had already overshadowed her in the Annunciation" (LG n. 59).

All of these give us a picture of someone who maintained her complete reverence for God and who constantly worked for the salvation of all those with whom she came in contact — throughout the ups and downs of her own life and against the background of the momentous transition from the Old to the New Testament. Throughout all of this she maintained a sense of balance, and so she is a "sign of sure hope and solace for the pilgrim people of God" (LG n. 68). Throughout all of this she lived that view of history seen not as an endless cycle of years but as the instrument of God for realizing His plan of salvation. And nowhere is this full Christian view of history more necessary than in regard to belief in and celebration of the Mass, especially in view of the momentous changes of the last several decades. As such, Mary is the model for calm acceptance of the workings of the Holy Spirit in history, whose meaning is not always immediately apparent to us.

This indeed is the spirit that will help us to recognize that it is

> a lack of historical perspective to canonize the liturgy of Vatican II as the final stage of liturgical development. The Church will continue to be a pilgrim subject to the changes and chances of time. Culture and thought will continue to influence her life and consequently her form of worship.[14]

And this is also to keep alive the spirit that has always characterized the Church at her best, which was so well expressed by Pope John XXIII in convening Vatican II:

> In the daily exercise of our pastoral office, we sometimes have to listen, much to our regret, to voices of persons who, though burning with zeal, are not endowed with too much sense of discretion or measure. In these modern times they can see nothing but prevarication and ruin. They say that our era, in comparison with past eras, is getting worse, and they behave as though they had learned nothing from history, which is, nonetheless, the teacher of life. They behave as though at the time of former Councils everything was full triumph for the Christian idea and life and for proper religious liberty.

> We feel that we must disagree with these prophets of gloom, who are always forecasting disaster, as though the end of the world were at hand.
>
> In the present order of things, Divine Providence is leading us to a new order of human relations, which by men's own efforts and even beyond their very expectations, are directed toward the fulfillment of God's superior and inscrutable designs. And everything, even human differences, leads to the greatest good of the Church.[15]

In this way Mary teaches us to be hopeful people — to see that liturgy is immersed in history but at the same time takes us beyond it.

4. Mary is also revealed in Scripture as a model of what it means to embody the *theological spirit* that should characterize every Catholic's participation in the Mass. For, after Jesus had been found in the Temple among the doctors of the Law, it is reported that Mary *stored up all these things in her heart* (Luke 2:52), and even if we have few words from Mary concerning the meaning of her participation in the Mystery of the Eucharist, her living out of it was quite clear. She is a perfect theologian in the sense that by her life she manifested Christ in His fullness — the incarnate Jesus, in the stable, to shepherds and Magi; the crucified Jesus, at the foot of His cross, to both believers and scoffers; the risen Jesus to fellow disciples of her Son by her prayerful presence with them, as recorded in Acts. This is as full a "handing on" of the Gospel and of the Eucharist as Paul speaks of doing (cf. 1 Corinthians 11:23;15:1). All Catholics, in imitation of Mary and the apostles, must look upon this "handing on" of Christ's message as an essential part of our life of faith. And an essential part of this is to engage in that prayerful pondering of these things in our hearts which is the theological enterprise. And Mary's life shows that this is not only a knowledge that is the product of an intellectual effort but a knowledge born of a life of faith, hope and love centered in the mystery of the Eucharist.

5. Finally, Mary is revealed in Scripture as a model of what it means *to participate fully in the Mass itself, in the Liturgy of the Word and in the Liturgy of the Eucharist.* For Mary was fully a part of Jesus' life — in word and deed — as He was a part of hers — from His conception to His crucifixion, from before His life on earth to after His return in glory to the Father and His Spirit's birth into the Church. And this unity of word and deed in her life, which remains a channel of grace for all men and women, was intimately bound up with her flesh and blood, for the "Son of God took a human nature from her, that He might in the mysteries of His flesh free man from sin" (LG n. 55). And that the birth of the Lord didn't "diminish his mother's virginal integrity" but rather "sanctified it" (LG n. 57) is witness to that mystery in which God is at the same time intimately united with His creation but also Lord of that same creation, which He is able to use as He desires (cf. Colossians 1:15-20). Also, however, this unity of word and deed in Mary's life is preeminently operative in the realm of faith, for: "This union of the mother with the Son in the work of salvation was manifested from the time of Christ's virginal conception up to His death" (LG n. 57). Indeed, even before the Word had become flesh in Mary's soul and body, Mary's role in the work of salvation had begun: *I will make you enemies of each other: you and the woman, your offspring and her offspring. It will crush your head and you will strike its heel* (Genesis 3:15). Mary's life is then what every prayer should be and what the Eucharist is in a preeminent way: a constant act of adoration, reconciliation, thanksgiving and intercession. And in the same way, our own humanity, united with the Eucharist, isn't in any way compromised or downgraded, but it is wondrously transformed into all it can be — fully united with God and one another.

Just as the Eucharist is not a luxury but a necessity for eternal life, so too is our full participation in the Mass a necessity, a necessity which has been laid out by *A CATHOLIC BOOK OF THE MASS* and a necessity which, in this last chapter, has found its perfect model in the Blessed Virgin Mary. We have talked much about why and how the Mass has been reformed, but this was only done so that the Mass might more efficaciously reform us and our world; that we will more completely offer ourselves along with Christ in His Sacrifice so that we will be able to celebrate His victory of grace over sin, of good over evil, of peace over conflict, of unity over division, of compassion over revenge and especially of love over hatred. For indeed, the Eucharist isn't so much a test of our faith and hope as it is of our love, and this temptation will intensify in the last days when the *love in most men will grow cold* (Matthew 24:12).

And this isn't surprising, since Scripture declares unequivocally that *God is love* (1 John 4:8), and this is what we have the most difficulty in accepting, as Julian of Norwich has pointed out:

> For some of us believe that God is almighty and may do all;
> and that He is all-wisdom and can do all; but that He is all-
> love, and will do all — there we fail.[16]

Yet, we Catholics needn't have any fear of failing in this way either, today or on the last day, since we always have the Eucharist in our midst. We have God embracing us, consoling us, strengthening us in a way that has never before been known or experienced by mankind. And the Eucharist alone can fully enable us to overcome our inability and slowness to love God and one another and ourselves and all creation with that fullness that characterizes divine love. For every day in our midst in the Mass we have a daily celebration of the belief that *nothing . . . can ever come between us and the love of God made visible in Christ Jesus our Lord* (Romans 8:38-39).

Chapter Eight: Discussion Questions

1. Discuss the relationship of the Blessed Virgin Mary to God's Plan of Salvation — to God, the Church, the Eucharist.

2. Discuss how the liturgy serves to make explicit much of what Catholics believe about the Blessed Virgin Mary.

Chapter Notes

Chapter One:

[1] Walter M. Abbott, S.J. (Gen. Ed.), *The Documents of Vatican II: The Constitution on the Sacred Liturgy (Sacrosanctum Concilium)*. New York: Guild Press, 1966, Article n. 23. (All future references to *The Constitution on the Sacred Liturgy* will be designated as e.g. *SC* n. 23 in the text of the book.)

[2] Abbott, op. cit., *Decree on the Ministry and Life of Priests (Presbyterorum Ordinis)*, Article n. 5. (All future references to the *Decree on the Ministry and Life of Priests* will be designated as e.g. *PO* n. 5.)

[3] Adrian Hastings, *A Concise Guide to the Documents of the Second Vatican Council*, Volume One. London: Darton, Longman and Todd, 1969, p. 106.

[4] *General Instruction of the ROMAN MISSAL (The Sacramentary)*, English trans., ICEL. New York: Catholic Book Publishing Co., 1974, Article no. 9. (All future references will be designated as e.g. *GI* n. 9.)

[5] *Ibid.* [6] *Ibid.* [7] *Ibid.* [8] *Ibid.*

[9] *Ibid.* [10] *Ibid.*, n. 10 [11] *Ibid.* [12] *Ibid.*

[13] Donald R. Campion, S.J., "The Church Today," (Introduction to *The Pastoral Constitution on the Church in the Modern World (Gaudium et Spes)*, in Abbott, *op. cit.*), pp. 185-186ff.

[14] Abbott, *op. cit., The Pastoral Constitution on the Church in the Modern World (Gaudium et Spes)*, Article n. 92. (All future references will be designated as e.g. *GS* n. 92.)

[15] Campion, *op. cit.*, p. 183.

[16] Abbott, *op. cit., The Dogmatic Constitution on the Church (Lumen Gentium)*, Article n. 16. (All future references will be designated as e.g. *LG* n. 16.)

[17] John Henry Newman, *Essay on the Development of Christian*

Doctrine, ed. and introduction, J.M. Cameron, 1845 edition. Middlesex, England: Penguin Books, 1974, p. 100.

[18]A.L. Maycock (ed.), *The Man Who Was Orthodox. A Selection from the Uncollected Writings of G.K. Chesterton*. London: Dennis Dobson, 1963, p. 149.

[19]P. Murray, "Liturgical Participation," *New Catholic Encyclopedia*. New York: McGraw-Hill Book Co., 1967, VIII: 907.

[20]St. John Chrysostom, "From a Homily on Matthew by St. John Chrysostom," *The Liturgy of the Hours*, trans. ICEL. New York: Catholic Book Publishing Co., 1975, vol. IV, p. 183.

[21]Abbott, *op. cit.*, Footnote n. 1 to LG n. 1, quoting Pope Paul VI, p. 14.

[22]C.J. McNaspy, S.J., "Liturgy," (Introduction to *The Constitution on the Sacred Liturgy (Sacrosanctum Concilium)*, in Abbott, *op. cit.*, p. 133.

[23]Anscar J. Chupungco, O.S.B., untitled article in *In Spirit and Truth*. Worship Commission, Diocese of Pittsburgh, September, 1984, p. 8.

[24]*GI* n. 15.   [25]*Ibid.*

Chapter Two:

[1]Ernest Lussier, S.S.S., *The Eucharist: The Bread of Life*. New York: Alba House, 1977, p. 85. [2]*Ibid.*

[3]Abbott, *op. cit., The Dogmatic Constitution on Divine Revelation (Dei Verbum)*, Article n. 21. (All future references will be designated as e.g. *DV* n. 21.)

[4]*The Teaching of Christ*, Ronald Lawler, O.F.M., Donald W. Wuerl and Thomas Comerford Lawler (eds.), 2nd ed. Huntington, Indiana: Our Sunday Visitor, Inc., 1983, p. 204.

[5]*Ibid.*   [6]Lussier, *op. cit.*, p. 60.

[7]Raymond Brown, S.S., *The Gospel According to John*, Anchor Bible Series, vol. 2. Garden City, New York: Doubleday and Company, Inc., p. 558.

[8]Brown, *op. cit.*, vol. 1, p. 287.   [9]*Ibid.*

[10]*Ibid.*   [11]*Ibid.*, p. 290.   [12]*Ibid.*   [13]*Ibid.*

[14]Lussier, *op. cit.*, Chapter Five.   [15]*Ibid.*, pp. 60-61, 70-71.

[16]Johannes Betz, "Eucharist: 1. Theological," *Sacramentum Mundi*, Vol. II. New York: Herder and Herder, 1968, pp. 257ff.

Chapter Three:

[1]John Navone, S.J., and Fr. Thomas Cooper, *Tellers of the Word*. New York: LeJacq Publishing Company, 1981, pp. 4-5.

[2]Joseph A. Jungmann, *The Early Liturgy to the Time of Gregory the Great*. London: Darton, Longman and Todd, Ltd., 1960, p. 1.

[3]*Ibid.*, p. 2.   [4]*Ibid.*   [5]*Ibid.*

[6]*Ibid.*   [7]*Ibid.*   [8]*Ibid.*   [9]*Ibid.*

[10]*The Mass.* Collegeville, Minnesota: The Liturgical Press, 1976, p. 17.

[11]A.G. Martimort, *The Church at Prayer. The Eucharist.* New York: Herder and Herder, 1973, p. 26.

[12]Theodor Klauser, *A Short History of the Western Liturgy.* Oxford: Oxford University Press, 2nd. ed., 1979, pp. 60ff.

[13]*Ibid.*, p. 77.   [14]*Ibid.*

Chapter Four:

[1]Pope Paul VI, *Encyclical Letter, Mysterium Fidei,* commentary by Anthony T. Padovano, S.T.D. Glen Rock, New Jersey: Paulist Press, 1966, Article no. 8. (All future references designated as e.g. *MF* n. 8.)

[2]Lussier, *op. cit.*, p. 231.   [3]*Ibid.*, p. 232.

[4]*The Teaching of Christ*, p. 168.

[5]Robert Bolt, *A Man For All Seasons.* New York: Random House, 1960, p. 141.

[6]Most Rev. John F. Whealon, "The Magisterium: Biblical and Pastoral Aspects," *L'Osservatore Romano* (Eng. ed.), quoting Pope Paul VI, April 13, 1978, p. 7.

[7]Edward Schillebeeckx, O.P., *The Eucharist.* London: Sheed and Ward, 1968, p. 19.

[8]Abbott, op. cit., *Decree on Ecumenism, (Unitatis Redintegratio)*, Article n. 17. (All future references will be designated as e.g. *UR* n. 17.)

[9]Helen Gardner, *Art Through the Ages*, 4th ed. New York: Harcourt, Brace and World, Inc., 1959, p. 283.

[10]H.A. Reinhold, "Allegorical Interpretation of the Liturgy," *New Catholic Encyclopedia*, Vol. VIII, p. 937.

[11]Joseph Powers, S.J., *Eucharistic Theology.* London: Herder and Herder, Inc., 1968, p. 30.

[12]Lussier, *op. cit.*, p. 223.   [13]Gardner, *op. cit.*, p. 284.

[14]Lussier, *op. cit.*, p. 45.   [15]*Ibid.*, p. 39.

[16]Leo Scheffczyk, "Eucharist: III. Eucharistic Sacrifice," *Sacramentum Mundi.* Herder and Herder, New York, Vol. II, p. 274.

[17]*Ibid.*   [18]Padovano, *op. cit.*, commentary, p. 16.

[19]Pope John Paul II, *Dominicae Cenae, L'Osservatore Romano* (Eng. Ed.), No. 12 (625), March 24, 1980, p. 6.

[20]Schillebeeckx, *op. cit.*, p. 97.   [21]*Ibid.*

[22]*Liddell and Scott's Greek-English Lexicon.* Oxford: Clarendon Press, 1963, p. 622.

[23]*Ibid.*   [24]Scheffczyk, *op. cit.*, p. 276.   [25]Schillebeeckx, *op. cit.*, p. 18.

[26]Pope John Paul II, "Nourish Your Spirituality and Catechesis with Dogmatic Truths", *L'Osservatore Romano* (Eng. Ed.), N. 23 (787), June 6, 1983, p. 3.

Chapter Five:

[1]"NCCB Commemorative Statement on the Liturgy," *Newsletter of the Bishops' Committee on the Liturgy* (NCCB), December, 1983, p. 1.

[2]*Ibid.*, p. 2.   [3]*GI* n. 6.   [4]McNaspy, *op. cit.*, p. 133.

[5]Joseph A. Jungmann, Introduction to the *Constitution on the Sacred Liturgy, Commentary on the Documents of Vatican II*, Vol. I, Herbert Vorgrimler (gen. ed.). New York: Herder and Herder, pp. 1-8.

[6]*Ibid.*   [7]*GI* n. 6.

[8]Pope Paul VI, "Apostolic Constitution: Promulgation of the *Roman Missal* Revised by Decree on the Second Vatican Ecumenical Council," *The Roman Missal* (*the Sacramentary*), English trans., ICEL. New York: Catholic Book Publishing Co., 1974, p. 8.

[9]N. Kollar, "Liturgical Participation," *Encyclopedic Dictionary of Religion*, Paul Kevin Meagher and others (eds.). Washington: Corpus Publications, 1979, pp. 2138-9.

[10]"Liturgiology," *Encyclopedic Dictionary of Religion*, p. 2143.

[11]Philip J. Rosato, "World Hunger and Eucharistic Theology," *America*, 135:3 (Aug. 7, 1976), p. 48.

[12]Joseph A. Jungmann, "Liturgy," *Sacramentum Mundi*, vol. III, p. 322.

[3]

Mitchell, "The Spirituality of Christian Worship," *Spirituality Today*, 34:1 (March 1982), p. 16.

Chapter Six:

[1]Martimort, *op. cit.*, p. 75.

[2]J.D. Crichton, *Christian Celebration of the Mass*. London: Cassell and Collier Macmillan Publishers, Ltd., 1971, pp. 71-2.

[3]*Ibid.*, p. 61.   [4]*Ibid.*, p. 72.   [5]Martimort, *op. cit.*, pp. 92-3.

[6]*Ibid.*, p. 96.   [7]*Ibid.*, p. 107   [8]Liddell & Scott, *op. cit.*, p. 486.

[9]Crichton, *op. cit.*, pp. 76ff.   [10]*Ibid.*, p. 79.

[11]Martimort, *op. cit.*, p. 109.   [12]*Ibid.*, p. 110.   [13]Crichton, *op. cit.*, p. 81.

Chapter Seven:

[1]Crichton, *op. cit.*, pp. 56-7.   [2]*Ibid.*, p. 56.

[3]Martimort, *op. cit.*, p. 118.   [4]*Ibid.*, p. 123.

[5]*Ibid.*, p. 121.   [6]*Ibid.*, p. 130.   [7]*Ibid.*, pp. 131-4.

[8]Crichton, *op. cit.*, pp. 84ff.   [9]Martimort, *op. cit.*, p. 135.

[10]*Ibid.*, p. 137.   [11]*Ibid.*, pp. 138ff.

[12]Joseph Martos, *Doors to the Sacred.* Garden City: Doubleday, 1981, pp. 255-6.

[13]Martimort, *op. cit.*, p. 162.   [14]*Ibid.*, pp. 154-5.

[15]Crichton, *op. cit.*, p. 88.   [16]Martimort, *op. cit.*, p. 156.

[17]*Ibid.*, p. 167.   [18]*Ibid.*, p. 171.   [19]*Ibid.*, p. 181.

Chapter Eight:

[1]Pope John Paul II, "At the Root of the Eucharist Is the Virginal and Maternal Life of Mary," *L'Osservatore Romano* (Eng.Ed.), N. 24 (788), June 13, 1983, p. 2 (Angelus of June 5, 1983).

[2]*Ibid.*   [3]*Ibid.*   [4]*Ibid.*   [5]*Ibid.*

[6]*Ibid.*   [7]*Ibid.*   [8]*Ibid.*   [9]*Ibid.*

[10]*Ibid.*   [11]*Ibid.*   [12]*Ibid.*

[13]Footnote in *LG*: St. Augustine, *De Sanctae Virginitate*, 6:PL 40,399.

[14]Anscar J. Chupungco, O.S.B., "A Historical Survey of Liturgical Adaptation," *In Spirit and Truth*, Worship Commission, Diocese of Pittsburgh, November 1981, p. 1.

[15]Pope John XXIII, "Pope John's Opening Speech to the Council," Abbott, *op. cit.*, pp. 712-713.

[16]Julian of Norwich, *The Revelations of Divine Love of Julian of Norwich*, trans. James Walsh, S.J. St. Meinrad, Indiana: Abbey Press, 1974, p. 188.

Bibliographies by Chapter

Chapter One:

Abbott, S.J., Walter M. (gen. ed.), *The Documents of Vatican II*. New York: Guild Press, 1966.

The Pastoral Constitution on the Church in the Modern World (Gaudium et Spes), in Abbott, *op. cit.*

The Dogmatic Constitution on the Church (Lumen Gentium), in Abbott, *op. cit.*

The Decree on the Ministry and Life of Priests, (Presbyterorum Ordinis), in Abbott, *op. cit.*

The Constitution on the Sacred Liturgy, (Sacrosanctum Concilium), in Abbott, *op. cit.*

Campion, S.J., Donald R., "The Church Today" (Introduction to *The Pastoral Constitution on the Church in the Modern World, (Gaudium et Spes)*, in Abbott, *op. cit.*

McNaspy, S.J., C.J., "Liturgy" (Introduction to *The Constitution on the Sacred Liturgy, (Sacrosanctum Concilium)*, in Abbott, *op. cit.*

St. John Chrysostom, "From a Homily on Matthew by St. John Chrysostom," *The Liturgy of the Hours*, trans., ICEL. New York: Catholic Book Publishing Company, 1975, Volume 4.

Chupungco, O.S.B., Anscar J., Untitled article in *In Spirit and Truth*, Worship Commission, Diocese of Pittsburgh, September 1984, pp. 1—8.

General Instruction on the Roman Missal (The Sacramentary), English trans., ICEL. New York: Catholic Book Publishing Company, 1974.

Hastings, Adrian., *A Concise Guide to the Documents of the Second Vatican Council*, Volume One. London: Darton, Longman and Todd, 1969.

Maycock, A.L. (ed.), *The Man Who Was Orthodox. A Selection from the Uncollected Writings of G.K. Chesterton*. London: Dennis Dobson, 1963.

Murray, P., "Liturgical Participation," *New Catholic Encyclopedia.* New York: McGraw-Hill Book Co., 1967, Vol. VIII: pp. 906-908.

Newman, John Henry, *Essay on the Development of Christian Doctrine,* ed. and introduction J.M. Cameron, 1845 edition. Middlesex, England: Penguin Books, 1974.

Chapter Two:

The Dogmatic Constitution on Divine Revelation (Dei Verbum), in Abbott, *op. cit.*

Betz, Johannes. "Eucharist: 1. Theological," *Sacramentum Mundi,* Volume II. New York: Herder and Herder, 1968, pp. 257-267.

Brown, S.S., Raymond, *The Gospel According to John,* 2 Volumes, The Anchor Bible Series. Garden City, New York; Doubleday and Company, Inc., 1966.

Lussier, S.S.S., Ernest, *The Eucharist: The Bread of Life.* New York: Alba House, 1977.

The Teaching of Christ. A Catholic Catechism for Adults, Ronald Lawler, O.F.M., Cap., Donald Wuerl, and Thomas Comerford Lawler (eds.), 2nd Edition. Huntington, Indiana: Our Sunday Visitor, Inc., 1983.

Supplementary:

Bouyer, Louis, *Eucharist.* Notre Dame: University of Notre Dame Press, 1968.

Brown, S.S., Raymond, *New Testament Essays.* Garden City, New York: Doubleday and Company, Inc., Image Books, 1968.

Cooke, Bernard, *Ministry to Word and Sacraments.* Philadelphia: Fortress Press, 1976.

Danielou, S.J., Jean, *The Bible and the Liturgy.* Notre Dame: University of Notre Dame Press, 1956.

Delorme, J., and others, *The Eucharist in the New Testament.* Baltimore: Helicon Press, 1964.

Tartre, S.S.S., Raymond A. (ed.), *The Eucharist Today. Essays on the Theology and Worship of the Real Presence.* New York: P.J. Kenedy and Sons, 1967.

Worden, T. (ed.), *Sacraments in Scripture.* Springfield, Ill.: Templegate, 1966.

Chapter Three:

Jungmann, S.J., Joseph A, *The Early Liturgy to the Time of Gregory the Great.* London: Darton, Longman and Todd, 1959.

———— *The Mass of the Roman Rite,* One Volume. New York: Benzinger Brothers, 1951.

Klauser, Theodor, *A Short History of the Western Liturgy.,* 2nd Edition. Oxford: Oxford University Press, 1979.

Martimort, A.G., *The Church at Prayer*. New York: Herder and Herder, 1973.

Navone, S.J., John, and Fr. Thomas Cooper, *Tellers of the Word*. New York: Le-Jacq Publishing Company, 1981.

Supplementary

Deiss, C.S.Sp., Lucien (ed.), *Early Sources of the Liturgy*. New York: Alba House, 1967.

Martin, Ralph, *Worship in the Early Church*. Grand Rapids, Michigan: William B. Eerdmans Publishing Company, 1964.

Martos, Joseph, *Doors to the Sacred*. Garden City, New York: Doubleday, 1981.

Chapter Four:

Decree on Ecumenism (Unitatis Redintegratio), in Abbott.

Bolt, Robert, *A Man for All Seasons*. New York: Random House, 1960.

Gardner, Helen, *Art Through the Ages*, 4th Edition. New York: Harcourt, Brace and World, Inc., 1959.

Pope John Paul II, *"Dominicae Cenae"* ("The Lord's Supper"), *L'Osservatore Romano* (Eng. Ed.), no. 12 (625), March 24, 1980, pp. 5-10.

———— "Nourish Your Spirituality and Catechesis with Dogmatic Truths," *L'Osservatore Romano* (Eng. Ed.), no. 23 (787), June 6, 1983, p. 3.

Liddell and Scott's Greek-English Lexicon. Oxford: Clarendon Press, 1963.

Pope Paul VI, *"Mysterium Fidei"* (commentary: Anthony J. Padovano). Ramsey, New Jersey: Paulist Press, 1966.

Powers, S.J., Joseph, *Eucharistic Theology*. London: Herder and Herder, 1968.

Reinhold, H.A., "Allegorical Interpretation of the Liturgy," *New Catholic Encyclopedia*, Volume VIII: 937-8.

Scheffczyk, Leo, "Eucharist: III, Eucharistic Sacrifice," *Sacramentum Mundi*. New York: Herder and Herder, Vol. II, pp. 273-6.

Schillebeeckx, O.P., Edward, *The Eucharist*. London: Sheed and Ward, 1968.

Whealon, Most Rev. John F., "The Magisterium: Biblical and Pastoral Aspects," *L'Osservatore Romano* (Eng. Ed.), April 13, 1978, pp. 5-7.

Supplementary

Carmody, John, *Theology for the 80's*. Philadelphia: The Westminster Press, 1983.

Crichton, J.D., *The Once and Future Liturgy*. Ramsey, New Jersey: Paulist Press, 1977.

Dulles, S.J., Avery, "The Symbolic Structure of Revelation," *Theological Studies* 41:1 (March 1980), pp. 51-73.

Empereur, S.J., James B., "Models for a Liturgical Spirituality," *The Sacraments*, Michael Taylor, S.J. (ed.), pp. 53-70.

Guzie, S.J., Tad W., *Jesus and the Eucharist*. Ramsey, New Jersey: Paulist Press, 1973.

Hellwig, Monika, *The Meaning of the Sacraments*. Dayton: Pflaum/Standard, 1972.

Martelet, Gustave, *The Risen Christ and the Eucharistic World*. New York: Seabury Press, 1976.

Vagaggini, O.S.B., Cyprian, *Theological Dimensions of the Liturgy*. Collegeville, Minnesota: The Liturgical Press, 1976.

Verheul, A., *Introduction to the Liturgy*. Wheathampstead, Hertfordshire: Anthony Clarke Books, 1972.

Chapter Five:

Code of Canon Law (trans.), Canon Law Society of America. Washington: Canon Law Society of America, 1983.

Jungmann, Joseph A., Introduction to the *Constitution on the Sacred Liturgy, Commentary on the Documents of Vatican II*, Vol. I, Herbert Vorgrimler (gen. ed.). New York: Herder and Herder, pp. 1-8.

———— "Liturgy," *Sacramentum Mundi*, Vol. III, pp. 320-331.

Kollar, N., "Liturgical Participation," *Encyclopedic Dictionary of Religion*, Paul Kevin Meagher and others (eds.). Washington: Corpus Publications, 1979, pp. 2138-9.

———— "Liturgiology," *Encyclopedic Dictionary of Religion*, p. 2143.

NCCB Commemorative Statement on the Liturgy, Newsletter of the Bishops' Committee on the Liturgy, NCCB, December 1983, pp. 1-5.

Mitchell, Nathan, "The Spirituality of Christian Worship," *Spirituality Today* 34:1 (March 1982), pp. 5-17.

Pope Paul VI, "Apostolic Constitution. Promulgation of the *Roman Missal* Revised by Decree of the Second Vatican Council," *The Roman Missal (The Sacramentary)*, Eng. trans., ICEL. New York: Catholic Book Publishing Co., 1974.

Rosato, Philip J., "World Hunger and Eucharistic Theology," *America*, 135:3 (Aug. 7, 1976), pp. 47-49.

Supplementary

Adam, Adolf, *The Liturgical Year*. New York: Pueblo Publishing Company, 1981.

Barauna, William (ed.), *The Liturgy of Vatican II: A Symposium in Two Volumes*. Chicago: Franciscan Herald Press, 1966.

Bouyer, Louis, *The Liturgy Revived*. Notre Dame: University of Notre Dame Press, 1964.

Braso, O.S.B., Gabriel, *Liturgy and Spirituality*. Collegeville, Minn.: The Liturgical Press, 1960.

Brown, Colin (gen. ed.), *The New International Dictionary of the New Testament*, Three Volumes. Grand Rapids, Michigan: Zondervan Publishing House, 1967.

Chapel, O.F.M., Paul, *A Living Liturgy*. New York: The Newman Press, 1967.

Champlin, Joseph M., *The Proper Balance*. Notre Dame: Ave Maria Press, 1981.

Collins, Mary, "Spirituality for a Lifetime," *Spirituality Today* 34:1 (March 1982), pp. 60-69.

Crichton, J.D., *Changes in the Liturgy*. New York: Alba House, 1965.

Emminghaus, Johannes H., *The Eucharist*. Collegeville, Minn.: The Liturgical Press, 1978.

Hovda, Robert, *Dry Bones*. Washington: Liturgical Conference, 1973.

Mitchell, Leonel L., *The Meaning of Ritual*. New York: The Paulist Press, 1977.

Rahner, Karl, "A Basic Interpretation of Vatican II," *Theological Studies* 40:4 (December 1979), pp. 716-27.

Ryan, Mary Perkins, *Has the New Liturgy Changed You?* New York: Paulist Press, 1967.

Searle, Mark, *Liturgy and Social Justice*. Collegeville, Minn.: The Liturgical Press, 1980.

Seasoltz, O.S.B., Kevin, *New Liturgy, New Laws*. Collegeville, Minn.: The Liturgical Press, 1979.

Taylor, S.J., Michael (ed.), *The Sacraments*. New York: Alba House, 1981.

———— and Romey P. Marshall, *Liturgy and Christian Unity*. Englewood Cliffs, New Jersey: Prentice-Hall, 1965.

Chapters Six and Seven:

Crichton, J.D., *Christian Celebration of the Mass*. London: Cassell and Collier Macmillan Publishers, Ltd., 1971.

Martos, Joseph, *Doors to the Sacred*. Garden City, New York: Doubleday, 1981.

Supplementary

Bishops' Committee on the Liturgy, *The Body of Christ*. Washington: National Conference of Catholic Bishops, 1977.

Champlin, Joseph M., *The Mass in a World of Change*. Notre Dame: Ave Maria Press, 1973.

———— *The New Yet Old Mass*. Notre Dame: Ave Maria Press, 1977.

Knox, Ronald, *The Mass in Slow Motion*. New York: Sheed and Ward, 1948.

McGloin, S.J., Joseph T., *How to Get More out of the Mass*. Liguori, Missouri: Liguori Publications, 1974.

Murphy, Charles, "Action for Justice Constitutive of the Preaching of the Gospel:

What did the 1971 Synod Mean?" *Theological Studies* 44:2 (June 1983), pp. 298-311.

National Conference of Catholic Bishops, *The New Eucharistic Prayers and Prefaces*. Washington: NCCB, 1968.

Walsh, S.S., Eugene A., *The Order of the Mass: Guidelines*. Glendale, Arizona: Pastoral Arts Associates of North America, 1979.

———— *Practical Suggestions for Celebrating Sunday Mass*. Glendale, Arizona: Pastoral Arts Associates of North America, 1978.

Chapter Eight:

Chupungco, O.S.B., Anscar J., "A Historical Survey of Liturgical Adaptation," *In Spirit and Truth*. Worship Commission, Diocese of Pittsburgh, November, 1981, pp. 1-12.

Pope John XXIII. "Pope John's Opening Speech to the Council," in Abbott, *op. cit.*

Pope John Paul II, "At the Root of the Eucharist Is the Virginal and Maternal Life of Mary," *L'Osservatore Romano* (Eng. Ed.), No. 24 (788), June 13, 1983, p. 2.

Julian of Norwich, *The Revelations of Divine Love of Julian of Norwich*, trans., James Walsh, S.J. St. Meinrad, Indiana: Abbey Press, 1974.

OTHER BOOKS FOR YOUR READING PLEASURE:

HOMILIES —

    FOR THE "A" CYCLE *No. 722, cloth, $14.95*

    FOR THE "B" CYCLE *No. 723, cloth, $14.95*

by Rev. John Jay Hughes

Based on the conviction that people are looking for hope and for a meaning to life, these homilies proceed from real-life situations, applying the biblical message and the Church's teaching to the lives of those in the pews

THE SUNDAY READINGS

by Rev. Albert J. Nevins, M.M.

A timely and functional examination of the theme for each Sunday Mass and how the readings relate to that theme. Assists in making the Mass more meaningful. Contains all the readings for all three yearly cycles and feast days. *No. 734, paper, $5.95*

PRAYER BOOK OF THE BIBLE: Reflections on the Old Testament

by Rev. Peter M. J. Stravinskas

Highly devotional book written as a scriptural guide to daily living. Representative passages are used as a daily source of solace and hope. Ideal for a better understanding of the Bible. *No. 606, paper, $4.95*

A LAY PSALTER

by Msgr. John Sheridan

Over 80 complete Psalms with meditations. Foreword by Timothy Cardinal Manning. Perfect as a source of prayer and meditation! *No. 716, paper, $7.50*

THE CHURCH YEAR IN PRAYER

by Rev. Jerome Neufelder

Using the Revised Standard Version, this delightful book combines Scripture, the 2,000-year Christian tradition and a contemporary understanding of prayer in the setting of the liturgical year. Perfect for cultivating personal prayer and the interior life. *No. 729, paper, $7.95*